# Calm

Few life skills are as neglected, yet as important, as the ability to remain calm. Our very worst decisions and interactions are almost invariably the result of a loss of calm – and a descent into anxiety and agitation. Surprisingly, but very fortunately, our power to remain calm can be rehearsed and improved. We don't have to stay where we are now: our responses to everyday challenges can dramatically alter. We can educate ourselves in the art of keeping calm not through slow breathing or special teas but through thinking. This is a book that patiently unpacks the causes of our greatest stresses and gives us a succession of highly persuasive, beautiful and sometimes dryly comic arguments with which to defend ourselves against panic and fury.

Published in 2016 by The School of Life
70 Marchmont Street, London WC1N 1AB
Copyright © The School of Life 2016
Designed and typeset by FLOK, Berlin
Printed in Latvia by Livonia Print

A proportion of this book has appeared online at thebookoflife.org.

Every effort has been made to contact the copyright holders of the
material reproduced in this book. If any have been inadvertently
overlooked, the publisher will be pleased to make restitution at the
earliest opportunity.

The School of Life offers programmes, publications and services to assist
modern individuals in their quest to live more engaged and meaningful
lives. We've also developed a collection of content-rich, design-led retail
products to promote useful insights and ideas from culture.

www.theschooloflife.com

ISBN 978-0-9935387-2-8

# Calm

# Introduction

Calm has a natural and deep appeal. Most of us long to be more patient, unruffled, at ease and capable of reacting with quiet good humour to life's setbacks and irritants.

But we are often still only at the very beginning of knowing how to be calm. Anxiety stalks us through our days and nights. It thrums almost permanently in the background. It may be with us now.

One response to agitation has become immensely popular in the West in recent years. Drawn from the traditions of Buddhism, this focuses on emptying the mind through the practice of meditation. The idea is to sit very quietly, perhaps in a special position, and strive, through a variety of exercises, to empty our minds of content. The aim is to push or draw away the disturbing and unfocused objects of consciousness to the periphery, leaving a central space empty, serene and minutely aware of itself.

Implicitly, this view proposes that a great many of the things we fret about are random and vain and that therefore the best solution is to still them; it suggests that our anxieties have nothing in particular to tell us. But there is another approach: one that interprets our worries as neurotically garbled, yet critical, signals about what may be amiss in our lives. In this school of thought, the point is not to try to deny or neuter anxiety, rather to learn to interpret it more skilfully, decoding certain valuable shards of information that our panicky moments are attempting to transmit to us – in admittedly very unfortunate ways.

Every failure of calm can be analysed in order to reveal something worth knowing about ourselves. Every worry, frustration, episode of impatience or burst of irritation has significant wisdom to reveal to us, so long as we take the trouble to decode it. Rather than strive to empty the mind, a favoured route to calm involves looking more carefully and slowly at our own agitated experiences with the aim of clarifying our underlying concerns.

This is the path of this book: in it we look systematically at a range of issues responsible for our agitations, furies and rages, unpicking the causes and listening to the content of our troubles, in order to reach a place of calm won through the patient and noble understanding of the curious byways of our minds.

Chapter One:

# Relationships

## i. Romantic Expectations

The central fantasy behind all the noise and anguish of relationships is to find someone we can be happy with. It sounds almost laughable, given what tends to happen.

We dream of someone who will understand us, with whom we can share our longings and our secrets, with whom we can be weak, playful, relaxed and properly ourselves.

Then the horror begins. We come across it second-hand when we hear the couple yelling at one another through the wall of the hotel room as we brush our teeth; when we see the sullen pair at the table across the restaurant; and sometimes, of course, when turmoil descends upon our own unions.

Nowhere do we tend to misbehave more gravely than in our relationships. We become in them people that our friends could hardly recognise. We discover a shocking capacity for distress and anger. We turn cold or get furious and slam doors. We swear and say wounding things. We bring enormously high hopes to our relationships – but in practice, these relationships often feel as if they have been especially designed to maximise distress.

A fundamental feature of the way our minds work is that we continually generate expectations about how things will go. Almost without noticing our tendencies, we draw up scenarios of how the future should unfold. These expectations are in no way innocent; they become the benchmarks against which we judge what actually happens. We deem something miserable or fantastic, not in and of itself but in relation to the notions of normality we have covertly assembled somewhere in our consciousness. We may thereby end up doing an acute injustice to the real conditions of our lives.

We're drawn into rages by situations that contravene what we expected would happen. We don't shout whenever things go wrong; only when they go wrong and we hadn't expected them to. It would be great if it could be sunny over the Easter break, but we have learned across long years that we live in a cloudy, generally damp, disappointing climate, so we won't stamp our feet when we realise it is drizzling. Once certain depressing situations have been budgeted for, we are at no risk of losing our tempers. We may not be happy, but we are not frothing. Yet when you can't find the car keys (they're always by the door, in the little drawer beneath the gloves), the reaction may be very different. Here, an expectation has been violated. Someone must have taken the damn keys on purpose. We were going to be on time, now we'll be late. This is a catastrophe. You are enraged because, somewhere in your mind, you have a perilous faith in a world in which car keys simply never go astray. Every one of our hopes, so innocently and mysteriously formed, opens us up to a vast terrain of suffering.

Romantic relationships have a habit of creating the highest kinds of expectation. The public realm is full of fantastical notions about what decades of life together with a partner could hold in store. We are no strangers to the challenges of love. We can observe people struggling all around us. Rates of divorce and incidents of domestic strife are avidly reported. Nevertheless, part of our minds remains remarkably impervious to the melancholy data. Despite a vast amount of evidence, we cling to notions of what love is like that bear little resemblance to any love story we have ever seen unfold anywhere near us.

We trust in our own plucky good fortune. Despite all the obstacles, we have faith that there is someone out there – the legendary 'one' – with whom everything will come right; someone with whom to bare one's soul and end one's days in deep satisfaction.

We aren't dreaming. We're just remembering. The origin of some of our hopes of love cannot be traced back to any adult experience. They can be identified with a slightly more curious source: early childhood. Our concept of what makes a happy couple is heavily influenced by the sort of relationship that an infant has with its parent, full of cosiness, wordless understanding and safety. Psychoanalysts suggest that we all knew the state of love in the womb and in early infancy when, at the best moments, a kindly caregiver interacted with us in a manner akin to that which a grown-up partner might employ with us. They ministered to our needs, even those we had trouble verbalising. They brought us a feeling of security and cuddled us to sleep. We are projecting a memory onto the future; we are anticipating what may happen from what once occurred according to a now-impossible template.

We have always had dreams of happy love. Only recently in history have we imagined that they might come to fruition within a marriage. An 18th-century French aristocrat would – for instance – take it for granted that marriage was a necessary matter for reproduction, property and social alliances. There was no expectation that it would, on top of it all, also lead to happiness with a spouse. That was reserved for affairs – the real targets of tender and complex emotional hopes. The practical sides of a relationship and the romantic longing for closeness and communion were kept on separate planes. Only very recently has the emotional idealism of the love affair come to be seen as possible, even necessary, within marriage. We expect, of course, that there will be major pragmatic dimensions to our unions, involving variable mortgage rates and children's car seats. But, at the same time, we expect that the relationship will fulfil all our longings for deep understanding and tenderness.

Our expectations make things very difficult.

The expectations might run as follows: a good lover generally understands us quite well, so it is unnecessary to spell out our inner states of mind at any length. At the end of stressful work routines, there is no need to specify that it would be nice to have some time alone: our lover will just know, and magically slip away upstairs. They will have an acute capacity to grasp what is going on inside us even if we have not used words to inform them. They will be very much on our side; they will see things from our point of view. They won't insist that we do certain things for them. Their needs will be minimal; they will have no annoying friends, and their family will be encouraging but unobtrusive.

Oddly enough, despite all the unsatisfactory relationships we may have had, we refuse to give up on our hopes. Experience seems unable to dent our expectations. Whenever we do fail,

we insist on attributing our setbacks to the particular character we got together with. We localise the problem: it was all
to do with the ex's strange habits and their refusal to grow
up as we told them to. We know how to be punitive about
our exes, yet refuse to blame love itself. We hold everything
responsible other than our ideas on love. And soon enough,
we are ready to gift our troublingly elevated expectations to
a new partner.

When we encounter difficulties in relationships, we are dis-
inclined to blame our ideas of love. We localise our troubles
instead. We focus on the particular flaws of the partner who
has undermined our Romantic expectations. We become ex-
perts in listing what is wrong with them – how they have let us
down, failed to understand us and been selfish. But we retain
a faith that someone, somewhere, might honour the hopes of
love that we cling to. It might be the person we met at the train
station who looked extremely charming in a camel-coloured
coat and with whom we exchanged a few words about the
vending machines. Perhaps they would be the answer. There
must be a better way than this.

We are seldom as vile as we are with the people with whom
we've agreed to share our lives. At the office and among
our friends, we are reliably kind and civil. Yet when we are
around the lover we've made more commitments to than to
anyone else on earth – the person named in our will, who
has a claim on our every possession – we show a bad temper
others could not imagine us capable of. We are not especially
evil or strange; it is our expectations that have made us so
tricky to be around. We can afford to be so friendly with our
acquaintances for a very simple reason: we just don't care
enough.

The person we love has unparalleled power to drive us to fury because there is no one of whom we expect more. Our most regrettable moments – swearing at them in the car, shouting late at night in the hotel, mocking their mannerisms at a party – are all the ghastly by-products of something superficially very innocent: hope, the most combustible and dangerous element of any relationship.

One way to calm ourselves down is to adopt a philosophy that, at first, sounds inimical to love: pessimism. We are used to thinking ill of this quality. It is redolent of resignation and cynicism. It seems the enemy of affection. Yet in love, it is precisely hope that endangers everything we might wish for.

The best way to enter a relationship should be to keep in mind the normality of being more or less constantly misunderstood. This should be no grounds for rancour or even surprise. Given how infinitely subtle and cavernous our minds are, it is no wonder if other people never manage to work out their contents. We would ideally calibrate our hopes accordingly from the start. We would know we are likely to remain largely unread even by those with the most tender intentions towards us. This doesn't mean we would always be miserable. Of course, especially in the early days, things truly would go well. Our lover would say something utterly in line with our most private beliefs. They would show an understanding of our deep selves beyond what even we could muster. But we would know that this would not be a regular occurrence. As time went on, we'd know that low-level misunderstanding would be the norm. We wouldn't get angry, or even surprised. From the first, our hopes would have been correctly calibrated. We wouldn't be bitter or defensive, just grateful for having known what to expect.

We'd ideally have an assumption that in any relationship there would be significant areas of disagreement – which could well turn out to be irresolvable. We wouldn't particularly relish this. It's not that we are eager to get together with someone with whom we are at odds. But we would just assume that we're not going to find someone who is on the same wavelength as us on every serious issue that crops up. The idea would be that a good relationship would involve strong agreement on a few pretty major matters, with the expectation that in a host of other areas there would be sharply divergent attitudes and ideas. This divergence wouldn't feel like a terrible climbdown or compromise. It would be normal, just as one would cheerfully work in an office alongside a person who had a totally different idea of what a nice holiday might be like or a bedtime unrelated to ours. We would know that a good working relationship would not mean blanket agreement. We'd be assuming that our partner would be quite often wrapped up in concerns of their own that wouldn't really have much to do with us.

In a wiser world than our own, we would regularly remind ourselves of the various reasons why people simply cannot live up to the expectations that have come to be linked to romantic relationships.

### The lover is not us
One of the striking features of babies is that, for a surprisingly long time, they have no secure sense that their mother is another person. She seems to be merely an appendage to their own being, like an extra limb that they almost – but don't entirely – control. Something of the same illusion accompanies us into adult relationships. Here, too, it can take a little while before we fully recognise that our lovers are not umbilically linked to our psyches; that they aren't extensions of us, but independent

beings with their own quite separate, and often painfully contrary, perspectives. They might be in a different mood to us, readying for bed just as we're getting excited to party, or hold contrary opinions on a film, or fail to sympathise with an idea that feels core to us.

## The start is no indication of what is to come

The feeling that we are 'in love' tends to begin with the realisation that we and the lover have an extraordinary amount in common. It might be very large things: political orientations; attitudes to education; views on the role of women in society. Or they might be much smaller yet still hugely significant matters: they too like long country walks, or early Baroque music, or the work of a little-known Bosnian poet. These discoveries create small bursts of ecstasy in lovers' hearts. They are redemptive signs of an end to loneliness.

The Romantic phase of love pivots around the recognition of what two people have in common, but the idea that this might be what love truly is, in and of itself, is a harbinger of an ill-tempered end to any union. If two people remain together, they will inevitably be confronted by areas of serious divergence. Far from being evidence that love is failing, the mapping of zones of difference is a sign that love has thrived and that two people are moving from the realm of unstable fantasy to that of noble and solidly founded reality.

## No one had a normal childhood

However well-meaning parents might be, no one ever has a 'normal' childhood in the sense of a set of experiences that leaves them ideally poised, ready to respond proportionately to difficulties, able to take challenges in their stride, disposed to a sanguine perspective on events – and able to love without ingeniously sabotaging the relationship they claim to be committed to. Such a creature is a theoretical possibility, of course, but he or she is unlikely ever to cross our paths.

Instead, we stumble on people who have been warped by dynamics that they neither understand properly nor can warn us about in good time. Perhaps they have a tendency to become furious for no apparent reason; perhaps our family evokes traumas for them that render them incapable of ordinary politeness in their company; maybe a stern father made them suspicious of all authority, or an over-indulgent mother made them unusually resistant to any form of criticism. They might have no ability to spend any time alone, or a hurtful proclivity for running upstairs to read a book at the first signs of tension.

We are liable to respond rather badly to the discovery of these warps, and to interpret them as evidence that we have been astonishingly unlucky. For a time, it seemed as if we had found someone normal, but in fact we have a freak (or worse) on our hands. We start to look around for alternatives. We zero in on the partner's flaws with manic accuracy. We are not wrong about these necessarily, but we are very wrong to imagine that they might not, in their general form, be universal.

Everyone is differently mad, but madness is general. The emergence of a human animal to maturity is too fraught a process to unfold without serious incident; therefore, distortions of character are a certainty rather than a risk. We should not wonder whether or not a prospective partner will be damaged; we need only consider how they might be so.

In many areas of culture and life, we can trace two major – and highly contrasting – attitudes, which can be summarised under the names 'Romantic' and 'Classical'. The distinction was first used in connection with the arts, but it readily applies to the way we think and feel about relationships. Many of our current expectations about what relationships are meant to be like are deeply influenced by Romantic ideas. There are several points of contention between Classicism and Romanticism, including:

### Authenticity vs politeness

From the late 18th century onwards, Romantic artists and thinkers got increasingly excited by the idea of speaking frankly and freely on all topics. They didn't like the idea of social convention constraining what they could or couldn't say. To hold back, they thought, was to be a kind of fake. To pretend to feel things you didn't really feel, to say something just because it would be nice for another person, was the mark of the hypocrite. Translated into relationships, this view has fed our expectations that we have to tell each other everything; that if we keep something back, we are betraying love.

By contrast, the Classical person reveres politeness. They see the point of smoothing things over even when there can't be total agreement, adding in the occasional artful stroke to the other's ego. It is not that they are afraid of ruffling anyone's feathers per se – but they feel it's not usually a constructive move. They sense that in reality we can only cope with a limited amount of negative or confronting news. And that to survive, a relationship may need to accept that there will be certain no-go areas, that there will be zones of privacy and resignation.

In the Classical view, the polite relationship isn't a painful compromise. It's not a climbdown from the too-difficult task of full openness. Rather it is a separate and distinct ideal of its own. The relationship should be a place where each person is conscious of how fragile their partner inevitably is on certain matters – and takes deliberate care to treat them delicately. This is an admired accomplishment and a real expression of love.

### Instinct vs rules

Starting in the arts, Romanticism tended to be very sceptical about training and learning lessons and was especially hostile to the notion of rules. No one, Romantics felt, could learn to be a poet or an artist; the arts were opposed to rules; success was a matter of having the right instincts and inspiration. By extension, the idea of learning how to be a lover or partner came to be seen as slightly repugnant.

By contrast, Classicism has embraced the notion of education very broadly. In the Classical view, one might need to be taught not just how to write a poem but how to have a conversation, how to be kind or how to deal with a relationship. Classicism builds on the idea that we're not naturally equipped to meet many of the major challenges of existence. We're coming to these difficult tasks with a serious shortfall of techniques. We are not naturally able to defuse a row, to say sorry or know how to share a kitchen. To the Classical mind these are crucial, learnable skills – and being taught them is no more embarrassing, and should be no more strange, than being taught to drive.

Attitudes to relationships are not universal and eternal. They are cultural creations. Though it's not a legacy we are consciously very much aware of, our current thinking is powerfully shaped by Romantic attitudes – which has resulted in some elevated expectations and subsequent panic and fury when they are not met. The Classical set of ideas about relationships operates with lower, less dramatic hopes about what good relationships are like – and carries a high regard for the qualities and skills that help us manage tensions. In search of calmer relationships, and happier loves, our collective attitudes should be heading in a more Classical, and politely more pessimistic, direction.

## ii. The Lack of Glamour of Domesticity

We are not blind to the idea that relationships might be hard. The issue comes down to where we think the difficulties might lie. Here the surrounding culture does us no service. The history of the Romantic novel, for example, is filled with examples of lovers battling against numerous obstacles. But these are of a particular sort: a pair of star-crossed souls may have to deal with the opposition of the Church or a faction in government. A devastating war may tear apart childhood sweethearts. Narrow-minded and snobbish parents may poison one partner against another. Romantic writers have shown genuine commitment to exploring a range of factors that can impede the development of love.

Nevertheless, one could accuse these Romantics of being unhelpfully selective about what particular problems they have focused on. It isn't that a war or a religious edict aren't serious; it's just that many other equally grave but also far more common challenges have tended to be ignored in their favour. Almost never has there been a Romantic novel that has meticulously studied the difficulties created for a couple by the issue of laundry. Seldom has a novel articulated the distress that can be caused by differences in ideas of a suitable bedtime, or the genuine agonies that emanate from kitchen cleaning rotas. We have, in art, seldom heard of a couple who broke up because one of the parties liked to play golf too much.

In part because of this oversight, couples are not sufficiently aware of the real flashpoints of love. They are therefore not prepared to devote the resources required to resolve everyday conflicts such as whether it is acceptable to eat in the bedroom, or if it is appropriately cautious to arrive at the airport four hours before a flight.

The more prestigious a problem, the more it attracts the patience and respect required to solve it. We can observe the benefits of this sort of humility in the world of science. Unlocking the secrets of the human genome was correctly viewed as immensely complex; those who set out on the task therefore approached their labour with fortitude, persistence and good humour. It was clear that this would not be an overnight win. The ability not to panic in a difficult situation hangs on our background awareness that difficulty is legitimate and expected. It helps immensely if the problems we face have a certain glamour to them. It is this that gives us the energy to attend properly to them, while what grinds down our spirits are problems that both bother us and give us the feeling that they are petty, trivial and not worth the attention of serious people. Without meaning to, the lack of focus on domestic life of which Romanticism is guilty has made us unnecessarily short-tempered around the scratchy reality of conjugal life.

We come into relationships with a host of ideas about what is normal. Without much thinking about it, you've maybe always just assumed that when having a meal, serving dishes should be placed on the table, so that you can help yourself. Then you get together with someone who's great in so many ways, but it turns out that they think it's really strange and annoying to put serving dishes on the table. To them, it seems obvious that you should really load up your plates at the stove and then sit down to eat. Like so many painful areas of conflict, it seems ridiculously minor when described coldly on a page. It's almost impossible to believe a couple could get frantic on a matter of this kind – such as, whether it's time to invest in a high-end new fridge or whether it is OK for one person to check up on the other's consumption of fruit and vegetables. Yet this is, in truth, the stuff of which all of our relationships are made.

When problems have not been given the attention they require, two members of a couple can fall into highly dispiriting roles: the nagger and the shirker. The nagger has given up trying to explain what is wrong or what needs to be done. They are no longer in the business of charming and good-naturedly cajoling. They merely insist and control. They give out orders rather than suggestions. Likewise, the shirker has given up framing their complaints in sensible terms. They just leave the room, shut their ears and bite their tongue in counterproductive ways. Both sides fail to explain the origins of their hurt and dissatisfaction.

In calmer lives, points of conflict and stress in domestic existence should be taken very seriously. They should have high prestige, in recognition of their complexity and role in the success of love. We should aim for a range of goals in this area:

### To increase patience

When we accept that an issue is intricate and serious, we are willing to be patient around it. If our partner doesn't have much insight into scuba-diving or the origins of the First World War, we don't throw up our hands in contemptuous despair. We take it for granted that these are matters on which a perfectly reasonable and decent person could be confused or ignorant.

### To make upset reasonable

If one's partner gets very agitated about which brand of olive oil to buy or how many sheets of toilet paper it is reasonable for one person to use in a day, it's easy to mock them and make them look ridiculous. But raising the prestige of the domestic means accepting that such details are matters on which a sane and sensible person could have strong feelings.

## To make disagreement legitimate

On many complicated issues it's going to make a lot of sense that there is more than one initially pretty plausible way of seeing them. After all, we accept that there might be more than one sensible approach to running a commercial aquarium or performing root canal surgery.

It can be strangely tricky for us to identify what kinds of tasks actually are hard – and therefore need to be approached with a lot of respect. A child learning to play the violin might get very worked up because they felt they were not making any progress – after twenty minutes. Failing to internalise that a challenge is going to be arduous is at the root of so many of our troubles. Gustave Flaubert went through his own version of painful education in the early days of his writing career. In his late twenties he was very keen to get established as a literary figure and he very rapidly wrote a novel, *The Temptation of St Anthony*. He asked various people for their opinion and the consensus was that he should throw the manuscript in the fire – which he did. He then set to work on his next novel – *Madame Bovary* – with a much more serious view of how hard the process would be and hence of how long it might take, and how often he would have to wrestle with a paragraph and change his mind about the flow of an individual sentence. It took him five years, but the novel was recognised as a masterpiece. There was a major reward for giving the details of writing a lot of attention.

Long-running, highly stressful domestic anxiety often circles around what look like pedantic details. What is the right way to cook a chicken? Should newspapers be kept in the bathroom? If you say you are going to do something 'in one minute', is it OK to actually do it eight minutes later? Is it extravagant to drink carbonated bottled water every day at home? They naturally provoke the thought that it is somewhat idiotic to get bothered about them. And so a path often recommended for a calmer relationship is that we should simply stop caring about such matters: that we should stop obsessing over details.

We can compare this attitude to the one we bestow on details in the arts. Here we know that details are hugely important and that we should give them special attention. The opening words of T. S. Eliot's *The Waste Land* – 'April is the cruellest month' could be changed to 'Of the months of the year, the most cruel is the fourth'. And it wouldn't really matter for the literal meaning. Normally it would be pedantic to make a fuss about the difference between 'cruellest' and 'most cruel' – or to get excited by the difference between 'April' and 'the fourth month of the year'. But in the poem, the exact vocabulary and sequence matter a lot. Eliot's phrase has a special character, sound and rhythm; it's blunt and harsh and it sticks in the mind. Something very similar goes on around painting – we don't get surprised if an artist ponders a precise tone of blue for half an hour. And we admire an architect for obsessing over the various textures of stone or slightly different tints of glass. In the arts, we acknowledge that small things – details – are densely packed with significance. Domestic details look small but carry big, important ideas. It might sound very odd at first to make the comparison, but the objects of domestic agitation are very like works of art: they condense complex meaning into tightly packed symbolic details.

In engineering, we take it for granted that a problem with something that looks tiny can have hugely serious consequences. We accept as obvious that a £300 million Airbus A380 – capable of taking hundreds of canapé-eating passengers serenely over the North Anatolian Mountains – can be rendered unusable by a tiny hydraulic leak in the landing gear. But we baulk at the notion that an adult – capable of managing the customer services division of an agricultural machinery supplier or teaching a class of fifteen-year-olds about the Vietnam War – can be rendered unable to function by the presence of toast crumbs on the butter or by the observation that it's a while since they last had a dental checkup.

Engineers aren't thrilled when a detail turns out to be a big problem, but they've usefully recognised that sorting out the little things is a completely legitimate and important part of the task. Art and engineering are places where we've collectively managed to recognise the importance of little things. Unfortunately, the very different cultural image we have of relationships – as being about big feelings, rather than little pragmatic issues – has made it hard for us to give these matters the serious attention they in fact deserve.

We might typically associate panic with the presence of a difficult task or an urgent demand. But that's not quite right. What actually causes panic is a difficulty *that hasn't been budgeted for* or a demand *that one has not been trained or prepared to meet*. The road to calmer relationships therefore isn't necessarily about removing points of contention. It's rather about assuming that they are going to happen and that they will inevitably require quite a lot of time and thought to address.

What would more ideally happen is a joint recognition from the earliest days that living with someone is one of the most difficult undertakings any of us ever assume. People may attempt the feat all the time, but this doesn't make it any easier or less grave. Properly equipped with an iron presumption of difficulty in our hearts, we would still hit problems, but our attitude towards them would change. We would not be so quick to deem them petty; we would be a little slower to anger; we might graciously spend hours discussing how to manage the bathroom or run the kitchen – and thereby help to rescue our relationships.

## iii. The Agitations of Sex

One of the assumptions of modern life is that getting the sex we want should be easy: we should be able to find someone we think both kind and attractive, we should be able to talk about our needs without awkwardness, we should have great sex across decades, we should know how to fuse desire with respect. We feel that happiness in this area is simply our due. We are consequently – and unsurprisingly – very unhappy around sex a lot of the time.

There are sweet moments – early on in relationships – when one person can't quite work up the courage to let another know just how much they like them. They'd love to touch the other's hand and find a place in their life; but their fear of rejection is so intense, they hesitate and falter. Our culture has a lot of sympathy for this awkward and intensely vulnerable stage of love.

The assumption, however, is that the terror of rejection will be limited in scope, focused on one particular phase of a relationship: its beginning. Once a partner finally accepts us and the union gets underway, the assumption is that the fear must come to an end. It would be peculiar for anxieties to continue even after two people had made some thoroughly explicit commitments to one another, after they had secured a joint mortgage, bought a house together, made vows, had a few children and named each other in their wills.

And yet one of the odder features of relationships is that, in truth, the fear of sexual rejection never ends. It continues, even in quite sane people, on a daily basis, and has some devastating consequences – chiefly because we refuse to pay it sufficient attention and aren't trained to spot its counter-intuitive symptoms in others. We haven't found a stigma-free, winning way to keep admitting just how much reassurance we need.

Within our psyches, acceptance is never a given, reciprocity is never assured; there can always be new threats, real or perceived, to love's integrity. The trigger to insecurity can be apparently minuscule. Perhaps the other has been away at work for unusual amounts of time; or they were pretty animated talking to a stranger at a party; or it's been a while since sex took place. Perhaps they weren't very warm to us when we walked into the kitchen. Or they've been rather silent for the last half an hour.

Yet even after years with someone, there can be a hurdle of fear about asking for proof that we are wanted. But with a horrible, added complication: we now assume that any such anxiety couldn't possibly exist. This makes it very difficult to recognise our feelings, let alone communicate them to others in ways that would stand a chance of securing us the understanding and sympathy we crave. Rather than asking for reassurance endearingly and laying out our longing with charm, we might instead mask our needs beneath some brusque and plainly hurtful behaviour guaranteed to frustrate our aims. Within established relationships, when the fear of rejection is denied, three major symptoms tend to show up.

Firstly, we get distant. We want to get close to our partners but feel so anxious that we may be unwanted, we freeze them out instead. We say we're busy, we pretend our thoughts are elsewhere, we imply that a need for reassurance would be the last thing on our minds.

We might even have an affair, the ultimate face-saving attempt to be distant – in a perverse effort to assert that we don't require the partner's love, which we have in fact been too reserved to ask for. Affairs can turn out to be the oddest of compliments: arduous proofs of indifference that we reserve for, and secretly address to, those we truly care about.

Secondly, we get controlling. We feel our partner is escaping us emotionally, and we respond by trying to pin them down administratively. We get unduly cross that they are a bit late, we chastise them heavily for not having done certain chores, we ask them constantly if they've completed a task they had agreed to undertake. All this, rather than admit: 'I'm worried I don't matter to you ...'

We can't force them to be generous and warm. We can't force them to want us – and we may not even have properly asked them to. So we try to control them procedurally. The goal isn't really to be in charge all the time, it's just that we can't admit to our terror about how much of ourselves we have surrendered. A tragic cycle then unfolds. We become shrill and unpleasant. To the other person, it feels like we can't possibly love them any more. Yet the truth is we do: we just fear rather too much that they don't love us.

Thirdly, we get nasty. As a final recourse, we ward off our vulnerability by denigrating the person who eludes us. We pick up on their weaknesses and complain about shortcomings. Anything rather than ask the question that so much disturbs us: does this person love and desire me? And yet, if this harsh, graceless behaviour could be truly understood for what it is, it would be revealed not as rejection, but as a strangely distorted – yet very real – plea for tenderness.

The solution to all this trouble is to normalise a new, and more accurate, picture of emotional functioning: to make it clear just how healthy and mature it is to be fragile and in repeated need of reassurance, especially around sex. We suffer because adult life posits too robust a picture of how we operate. It tries to teach us to be implausibly independent and invulnerable. It suggests it might not be right to want a partner to show us they still really like us after they have been away for only a few hours. Or to want them to reassure us that they haven't gone off us – just on the basis that they haven't paid us much attention at a party and didn't want to leave when we did.

And yet it is precisely this sort of reassurance that we constantly stand in need of. We can never be through with the requirement for acceptance. This isn't a curse limited to the weak and the inadequate. Insecurity is, in this area, a sign of well-being. It means we haven't allowed ourselves to take other people for granted. It means we remain realistic enough to see that things could genuinely turn out badly – and are invested enough to care.

We should create room for regular moments, perhaps as often as every few hours, when we can feel unembarrassed and legitimate about asking for confirmation. 'I really need you; do you still want me?' should be the most normal of enquiries. We should uncouple the admission of need from any associations with the unfortunate and punitively macho term 'neediness'. We must get better at seeing the love and longing that lurk behind some of our and our partner's most frosty, managerial and brutish moments.

If we consider sex in isolation, the hope of finding an ideal partner, with whom it would be easy to announce the full range of one's erotic curiosity, sounds plausible. One could perhaps find someone who wants to use fur-lined handcuffs and running shoes – as we do (let's imagine). But that's only a small corner of the problem. Because, in a relationship, the hope is that this same person will also be interested in our views on politics and culture, our attitudes to mealtimes and the colour for the downstairs bathroom. There are many facets of sexual excitement that are simply genuinely at odds with other aspects of our nature, with our hopes for love – and with being an otherwise decent and nice individual. Erotic excitement doesn't take note of the standards that we've defined for ourselves in the rest of our life. It really is a very strange transition we have to make in company with another person: to go from making polite enquiries as to the merits of an entrée or advancing a critique of American electoral politics, to attempting to tie a person up and defile them. We need to be modest about how we can reconcile all aspects of ourselves in the company of one other unique individual.

For people who have been together for a long time, it can get increasingly difficult to separate sex from the domestic realm. Someone who is seeking to assert themselves about a major financial matter, or tries to impose their ideas about a holiday, can find it very difficult to then change gear in bed in order to dare to be more passive and submissive. They might really want to, but feel they couldn't afford to put so much vulnerability on display.

Our sex lives developed in complex ways long before any given relationship. Each person's sexual character is gradually shaped and developed over many years, influenced by a range of elements picked up from childhood onwards: the cover of a fashion magazine; key scenes in films; the words of a song their brother liked; someone dancing at their cousin's wedding; their mother's haircut … The sexual persona starts to take shape before we have anyone to share it with, deep in the privacy of our own imagination. It's a private language that no one else knows how to speak. Conveying it to another person – getting another person to make sense of you sexually – really is a very delicate and difficult operation. We might have to retrace with them the long, half-forgotten episodes of how we came to be the sexual person we are today. All this sits very uneasily with the feeling that great sex should be spontaneous, dramatic and wholly passionate.

For several decades, sex has occupied an incredibly prestigious place in the modern idea of a good life, a vision of existence continually impressed upon us by some of the most powerful cultural forces of our times: advertising, music and online porn. Until the 1960s, the idea of following one's sexual impulses wherever they might lead still seemed deeply shocking. Even very intellectual and oblique expressions of this attitude (such as James Joyce's *Ulysses* or D. H. Lawrence's *Lady Chatterley's Lover*) were rigorously suppressed. The established view, at that time, was that sex was a dangerous, dark, rather tragic element, to be treated with great caution. The expectation of getting what one wanted from sex for any length of time simply never arose.

We've come to inhabit the opposite kind of society, one in which it seems shocking to imagine not having a deeply interesting and fulfilling erotic life that dovetails precisely with a domestic and emotional union that lasts for a lifetime. The positive view has come to feel completely standard. But it carries a fiendish problem with it, for it doesn't take into account the many very real obstacles to its realisation. So it brings – wholly without meaning to – a new source of panic and dismay. We would be a great deal calmer if we started from the assumption that there will by definition need to be a great deal of renunciation in our sexual lives. The best route to a so-called 'good' sex life is to honour the idea that great sex will almost certainly be the occasional ecstatic exception in a life otherwise filled with compromise and frustrated desire.

## iv. The Weakness of Strength

We tend to like people for what is good about them. That's what brings us together. If a friend asks you what you see in a person you are starting a relationship with, you will point to some lovely things about them. Maybe they are really neat around the kitchen and you are really enjoying the feeling that everything is under control and beautifully organised. Or maybe they are very flirtatious and playful and it's great fun being around them; at parties everyone thinks they are fascinating and you're proud to be with someone so socially adept. Or else it could be that they have a really charming rebellious streak: they don't care much what others think, they just get on and do their own thing. If they don't much like a job they'll chuck it in, and on the spur of the moment they'll head off camping for the weekend or invite eight people they met in the pub round for a late-night drinking session.

But as a relationship continues, we become more and more obsessed with our partner's failings. And there's often a fiendish irony at work: the things that madden us turn out to be connected to the very qualities that were initially part of their appeal. The unpredictability of the spontaneous person starts to infuriate. The always-neat kitchen can become the focus of what feel like exorbitant demands. The social star starts to bring on feelings of insecurity.

What we're looking at here are instances of a major law of human nature: the principle of the Weakness of Strength. This states that any good quality a person has, will, in some situations, be revealed as accompanied by a corresponding weakness. Someone who is excitingly creative and imaginative will quite probably turn out to struggle with routine practical tasks. Someone who is impressively focused on work will, for that very reason, often feel compelled to put the demands of their job ahead of your interests and needs. A person who is a highly sympathetic listener will at times be indecisive because they are so ready to see the merits of opposing sides. The highly charged, sexually adventurous individual will struggle with fidelity. The great conversationalist might want to stay up talking till three in the morning and react very badly to being reminded that they have to get up early to take the children to kindergarten.

Keeping in mind the idea of the inevitable weaknesses that accompany a person's strengths can help us be calmer in relationships. It offers us a less alarming and less upsetting interpretation of the genuinely disappointing things our partners do. When the other person annoys us, there's a strong tendency to see this part of their behaviour as something they could easily stop. Why don't they just ease up on their obsession with perfectly wiped work surfaces? Why don't they take more time off? Why don't they come to bed early? Why don't they get more focused on their career? These questions rattle around in our heads and we answer them for ourselves in rather grim terms. It's because they don't care about us as a couple; it's because they are mean; it's because they are obsessive or cold or selfish or weak. We view their actions as the result of some really awful things about them that they could change if only they wanted. It feels as if they are deliberately setting out to thwart us.

This way of seeing a partner's failings makes us painfully agitated. The Weakness of Strength theory reminds us that many of our partner's irritating and disappointing characteristics are actually the shadow sides of things we really like about them.

We should make a list of their most annoying tendencies and ask ourselves in each case: what good thing is this painful trait connected to? There will be some for sure.

Suppose, if you are going to the airport, that they always want to set off very early. They keep telling you to hurry up and get out the door when you know there's actually plenty of time. It drives you crazy because you end up having to hang about for ages at the departure lounge. Your instinct is to feel that they are dictatorial and stupid; why can't they relax and be nice? You feel like dragging your heels or shouting at them not to be so ridiculous. They get more and more distressed, and so do you. Alternatively, you could try to identify the underlying good quality that – unfortunately – is showing up as a weakness just here. In other areas, this person is very reluctant to leave things to chance, which is a real asset. If they say they'll do something, you can be pretty sure they will; if you arrange to meet them, they'll show up on time. They turn out to be very good at organising your joint social life and the fridge is always well stocked.

The shift in interpretation doesn't make the annoying fault go away, and it doesn't mean there's nothing this person could ever do in terms of self-improvement. But it does mean that we're no longer staring at an utterly bleak internal vision of who our partner might be. They've not turned into a monster – the constant anxiety-inducing thought that dogs relationships. They are a nice person who is just now showing the negative sides of a good quality.

Every so often you are likely to come across a new person who seems, in some ways, much nicer than your current partner. You meet them at a party and they are very funny and engaging. Or they are teaching on a course you're attending and you see how patient they are. There's a neighbour who is often looking after their garden and you like their nurturing style – and how they look in an old jumper. We get infatuated with such people. We imagine how lovely it would be to be with them. And this makes us more and more irritable around our own partners.

The Weakness of Strength idea suggests, though, that we should get clear in our heads that the very nice qualities of this new person will – at some crucial stage – also be connected up to maddening bits of behaviour. We may not know how they will madden us, but we can be sure that they will. We should learn to ask ourselves, before giving way to a crush, how the really nice sides of strangers could become a problem. Patience is wonderful, but at some point this person is going to appear passive. They'll be being patient when you really need to hurry. They'll have long chats with people in shops while you are aching to get away. The gardener will always be heading out to trim the beds or check for snails early in the morning, when it would be lovely to be cosy with them in bed. We don't know what exactly the problems will be. But we should be entirely certain that there will be many.

In May 1787, the German poet and statesman Johann Wolfgang von Goethe was taking a boat from Sicily to the Italian mainland. A lot of passengers were making the short trip. The wind failed and a strong current started to push the boat towards the rocky cliffs. Everyone could see what was happening. The captain and the crew were desperately trying to dismantle the mast of the ship and use it to fend themselves off from the approaching rocks. But their efforts – Goethe noted – were severely hampered by the panicked passengers getting in the crew's way and screaming at the captain to do something, so that he had to give his attention to trying to quieten them down rather than focusing on the safety of the ship. Goethe tried very hard to pacify his fellow passengers, because it was obvious to him that their agitation was a real threat to everyone's safety.

It's a situation that's representative of the problem of agitation in our own lives. Our panic has a fatal way of undermining our capacity to deal with the underlying, real problems. Being calmer doesn't at all mean that we think everything can be fine; it just means we are in a better state of mind to cope with the genuine challenges of our lives. And in Goethe's case it worked. The captain was able to put his plan into action; the sailors managed to hold the boat off from the rocks long enough for the wind to revive – at which point they could hoist sail, make headway against the current and reach their destination unharmed.

Chapter Two:

# Other People

## i. Unintended Hurt

The capacity to stay calm is, to a critical extent, subject to our ability to keep in mind the difference between harm that is intentional and harm that is accidental. Most legal systems around the world honour the difference, distinguishing (for example) manslaughter from murder. The degree of damage may be the same whichever motive is involved, but it matters hugely in the eyes of the law and of the public what intention was at play. This is eminently cautionary – and logical. If an explicitly evil intention is at large, it needs to be contained and controlled, for it may wound someone again. However, if harm was only an accident, then an explanation and apology will be all that is required to make amends and restore the peace.

We can imagine ourselves in a smart restaurant. The waiter serving us tips tomato sauce all over our freshly dry-cleaned suit. Our immediate response is to shout at him. But one side of our minds will be scanning for evidence of whether this harm was accidental or intentional – and therefore whether it would be fair to become incensed or to be kind and reasonable enough to forgive. Were the waiter immediately to show heart-felt concern and sincere apology, it would be fitting to shrug off the damage and even sympathise with them for the difficulty and occasional risks of their employment.

The intentions that are in operation are therefore of critical importance. Sadly, we are notoriously bad judges of other people's intentions. We are liable to interpret relative innocence or even plain happenstance through a lens of dark suspicion. As a result, we turn mere problems into grave disputes and enduring resentments.

Our proclivity for interpreting dark plots against us can be traced back to a problem for which we deserve compassion: we don't like ourselves very much. This background of self-contempt immediately leads us to suspect that others are out to get us. Why, after all, would they be any nicer to us than we are to ourselves? When we see ourselves as legitimate targets for hurt, it appears almost natural that, the moment we settle down to work, a drill should start up outside; or that when we urgently need to get to a meeting, the roads should be clogged up with traffic. These problems are evidence of a world conspiring against someone it knows to be an unattractive participant deserving of constant punishment. We are getting what we are owed.

Not liking ourselves can inspire a constant search for an echo in the outer realm of what we feel to be true of us in the inner one. We will scan the horizon for any evidence of the negativity that we bear within ourselves. The origins of the problem lie, as ever, in childhood, where our caregivers or families endowed us with a sense of being worthless and undeserving. It is this hinterland of psychological self-hatred that explains our haste to assume the worst; not because the worst will be true, but because it feels familiar and deserved.

A reason why others may unintentionally harm us is that we often look rather strong from the outside. We may not even be aware of how skilled we have become at putting up a cheerful, robust façade around others. It's something we perhaps learned in our early adolescence, at about the time we started at the new school. While often an advantage, it can lead people to say tough and hurtful things – without really meaning to. They just don't know how bruised and fragile we already are. They don't grasp just how big an impact on us their words or actions can have, because they don't know – and can't really know – how vulnerable we already are in our psyches.

Someone might come up to you at work and give a pretty unflattering assessment of a presentation you made. They mean to make some sort of impact. They want you to notice a bit. But from your side it feels very different. It's deeply, catastrophically upsetting. You'd been nervous beforehand – now this! In another role last year you'd had some problems and had seen a life coach. In this new job, you'd been determined to lift your game. Your self-respect was already bruised. And your father was especially critical of the way you spoke, mocking the slight lisp you had before the age of eight. But others can't tell all this. You don't look especially at risk. You're like a vase with tiny cracks you can hardly distinguish. Yet even a minor jolt will make the whole thing fall apart.

Ideally we would be able to give other people early warning of our areas of fragility, so that they could take this into account when dealing with us. We're pretty ready to do this around physical bruises and injuries. If you have a bandaged hand, people know not to grab it. And in theory the same could happen with tender psychological areas.

Yet it can feel too shameful and convoluted to explain to others just how many cracks we are already carrying. There's no time. And in any case the reasons may not reflect well on us. We're perhaps fragile because we wasted a lot of money; because we're having an affair and feel deeply guilty and terrified we're going to get found out; because we've been watching so much online pornography we feel disgusted at ourselves. We feel we're burdened and can only just keep going, and yet we can't often really let other people know why. And so we are faced with a torturous dilemma: people will cause us a lot more distress than they ever meant to, given who they thought we were.

Secret fragility – the cracks that have been accumulating over days, weeks and years – explains our occasionally extraordinary outbursts that can be so puzzling to onlookers. An apparently tiny remark unleashes a furious response from us. Imagine we are paying at the local corner shop and the total is a bit more than we'd been assuming it would be. Instantly, we feel that the person at the till is trying to cheat us. We hand them a note and they take a bit longer counting out the change and we suddenly say, angrily, 'Just keep it', and make a grimace and storm out, crashing painfully into a large tub of new potatoes as we do so.

Young children can be deeply testing to be around. We may display heightened care and devotion towards them, yet our efforts stand to be ignored and trampled upon in dramatic ways. We might come home early from work and carefully cook them a meal of chicken and potatoes, but find that they angrily push the plate on the floor and say, 'I hate you.' It hurts, but we stay composed and look for attenuating circumstances. Maybe they have toothache; maybe they are jealous of their younger sibling; maybe they didn't sleep well the night before. We are primed to seek gentle explanations to take the edge off some of the most dispiriting behaviour of children, and, by doing so, are prevented from a run of violent crises.

Our equanimity around children contrasts markedly with our agitation around adults. Here we are unlikely to look for attenuating explanations when bad behaviour strikes. We immediately assume that whatever has hurt us must spring from the worst motives. We are unlikely to wonder whether the snappy remark or the banged door have been caused by lack of sleep or agitation around a tricky boss. We don't – as we wisely do with a four-year-old – ask if someone else is annoying them and they are using us as a safe dumping-ground: this is hardly edifying behaviour, but understandable in the compromised conditions of ordinary life. If we used our imaginations a little more actively, our partner's antics wouldn't magically cease to affect us, we wouldn't grow impervious, but our ability to remain calm around them would be markedly improved. Almost all of us are kind around children, and yet comparatively still so unkind around the immature aspects of our adult selves.

One of France's greatest 20th-century philosophers was Émile-Auguste Chartier (known as Alain). Much of his writing is taken up with analyses of intolerance. In one especially memorable passage, Alain asks his readers never to say that people are evil or bad. Instead, we should always 'look for the pin'. What Alain meant by 'the pin' was the thing in someone's life that prompts them to behave in apparently evil and unkind ways. It might be a physical illness, jealousy of a colleague, or lack of respect from the world. The point is that the pin is external to the person who is behaving badly. It is affecting them, but it is not them – and if it were removed, the person would show their true nature, which (as Alain imagined it) is likely to be essentially kind, tolerant and generous. We are not bad in and of ourselves; we end up bad because there is a sharp object poking us in a tender place. To keep this always in mind is to arm ourselves against immediate retaliation and rage. Our so-called enemies are not outright knaves. They are nice people labouring under a pain they cannot explain to us or overcome in themselves. They are to be pitied rather than hated. This is the move that great novelists know how to make. Dostoevsky, for example, looks behind the off-putting façades of his characters (prostitutes, murderers, addicts) and sees the suffering human who deserves our compassion.

To show this sort of imagination, to picture for ourselves what is going on inside the minds of people whom it would be easy to dismiss, is not just a response we see in great fiction. It is the work of love. And it is a move we need constantly to rehearse around those we live with. We too need to look behind surface aggression and contempt and piece together for ourselves the pain that must be at play. We need to direct our kindness in the most counterintuitive direction: towards those who frustrate us most acutely.

## ii. In Defence of Teaching

We constantly get hugely irritated and upset by the fact that people don't understand or grasp crucial things that we need them to know. We end up seething with resentment at their ongoing ignorance (the way to format an introductory letter, the best way to budget, why the bedroom window should be closed) – and in response, we lose all calm and capacity for kindness.

More particularly, and paradoxically, we are often furious at them for not knowing something that we assume they should know – *without ever having been taught it*. And we have not taught them what we are convinced they must know for a fundamental reason: because we don't respect teaching very much.

In theory, we respect teachers; we pay lip service to the concept of education, but in practice, teaching may feel like a dull unworthy sort of occupation. It bored us for years at school and now we tend to be happy to leave it to other, lesser mortals. And yet teaching is one of the most central, unavoidable and, in many ways, noble aspects of life. Even if we haven't signed up to instruct adolescents in maths or languages, even if we aren't interested in telling someone how to find the area of a circle or ask for a train ticket in French, we are called upon to 'teach' almost every hour of every day: teach others how we're feeling, what we want, what is paining us, the way we think things should be. The teaching specialisation we have to take on is a bizarre-sounding but crucial subject: *Who I Am and What I Care About*. Yet, in so many areas, we rush over the curriculum and skip to the punishment phase. We fail to get others to see what matters so much to us: why we were hurt by that sarcastic remark over dinner, why we are maddened when people speak out of turn at a meeting, why it wouldn't be a good idea to pull together a committee to explore the proposal. We've fatally misconstrued teaching as a specific professional job, when in actuality it's a basic psychological manoeuvre upon which the health of every community, relationship and office depends.

'Teaching' is the infinitely complex art of getting an idea, insight, emotion or skill from one human brain into another. Whatever the subject matter, the core requirements for this tend to be the same, the first and foremost among them being that the 'student' should not be scared. We rarely learn very well when we have been humiliated or belittled, are insulted and threatened. Few of us can take ideas properly on board when we have been called fools and shits. Our minds are simply not at their most receptive until we have been patiently comforted, reassured of our value and given licence to fail.

The second core-related requirement is that the teacher not panic. A hysterical teacher has a priori lost the capacity to accomplish their goals. It's a paradox of the field that our teaching efforts tend to succeed the less manically we care that they will come off. Being in a position not to mind too much if our lessons haven't really had the desired impact can be the best way of ensuring that we will stay patient with the student – and thereby succeed. A sense that everything is at stake and the world is ending – easy enough impressions to reach in relationships and at work – guarantees to turn us into catastrophic pedagogues.

The good teacher knows that timing is critical to successful instruction. We tend automatically to try to teach a lesson the moment the problem arises, rather than when it is most likely to be attended to (it might be several days later). And so we typically end up addressing the most delicate and complex teaching tasks just at the point when we feel most distressed and our student is most exhausted or nervous. We should learn to proceed like a wily general who knows how to wait for just the right conditions to make a move. We should develop a cult of great timing in addressing tricky matters, passing down stories from generation to generation of how, after years of getting nowhere with impulse-driven frontal assaults, a great teacher stood patiently by the dishwasher until her partner had put down the newspaper, reflected on the upcoming holidays, and then carefully advanced her long-prepared point, and eventually won a decisive teaching victory.

Too often, we are annoyed not only that we have to teach, but that our 'student' doesn't yet know, given their education, background, salary ... We carry a heavy background grudge that someone doesn't yet know something they have never been given a chance to learn. So great is the intensity of disappointment, it cuts us off from the poise necessary to educate them into respecting (and then perhaps living up to) one's vision.

We are the unconscious inheritors of a Romantic tradition that encourages suspicion of teaching outside of narrowly technical fields. It can sound weird or impossible to have to try and teach someone to be less cheerful in their documents, to alter their response to new ideas or to approach difficulty with greater resilience. We fail because we're not alive to the scale, possibility and dignity of the teaching task.

When we give up on teaching (and, therefore, on those we need to teach), we tend to manoeuvre around the objects of our despair. We tell them their work is OK, but silently redo it with other colleagues. We set up secret side groups. It's meant to be a collaboration between twenty equals. But we go out and hire two external consultants. It sounds Machiavellian – but it's merely the outcome of a very nervous personality with low faith in others and in the chances of working through problems. In their personal lives, such types might be married but seek a lover: for they have areas of disappointment and anger they have never found ways of discussing – and it seemed better to steer around the conflict and take a lover to soak up some of the disappointment. In business, too, they may be devoting themselves to 'lovers' because they can't tolerate the tensions and ambiguities of sticking with the group they've originally pledged themselves to. Secret manoeuvring is a vote of no-confidence in the possibilities of persuasion or education. It's the result of a big conclusion somewhere in the mind: that nothing good can come from dealing with people directly.

We don't often think about it – and may never discuss it with others at all – but pretty much everyone has voices in their heads: a murmuring stream of thoughts that run along inside our minds most of the time. Sometimes the inner voice is encouraging, calling for us to run those final few yards: 'You're nearly there, keep going, keep going.' Or it is urging us to calm down, because we know it will all be OK in the end. But sometimes the inner voice is simply not very nice at all. It is defeatist and punitive, panic-ridden and humiliating. It doesn't represent anything like our best insights or most mature capacities. It's not the voice of our better nature. We find ourselves saying: 'You disgust me, things always go to shit with you.' Or: 'You useless little idiot.' Where do inner voices come from? An inner voice always used to be an outer voice. We absorb the tone of others: a harassed or angry parent; the menacing threats of an elder sibling keen to put us down; the words of a school-yard bully or a teacher who seemed impossible to please. We internalise the unhelpful voices because at certain key moments in the past they sounded compelling. The authority figures repeated their messages over and over until they got lodged in our own way of thinking. Part of becoming a good teacher means altering how we speak to ourselves – and then, in turn, others. To do this we need to encounter equally convincing and confident, but also helpful and constructive, varieties of voices over long periods – and take care to internalise them: the voices of a friend, a therapist, an author or a kindly teacher. We need to hear the voices often enough and around tricky enough issues that they come to feel like natural responses; they become our own thoughts that we can then speak to others about. The best sort of inner voice addresses us in a gentle and unhurried way. It should feel as if a sympathetic arm were being put around our shoulder by someone who had lived long and seen a great many sad things but wasn't embittered or panicked by them. In the worst moments of anxiety at work, there may be a mocking and contemptuous voice inside one's head, suggesting that love, respect and kindness only ever come via worldly success and competence. We feel that failure (not being able to make the team work, get on top of things, eradicate sloppiness) rightly debars us from love and appreciation. We need to incorporate a voice that separates out achievement from love: that reminds us that we may be worthy of affection even if we fail and that being a winner is only one part, and not necessarily the most important part, of one's identity.

This is – traditionally – the voice of the mother, but it might also be the voice of a lover, a poet we like or our nine-year-old child. It is the voice of a person who loves you for being you, outside of achievement. Many of us grew up around nervous people who lost their tempers the moment the parking ticket couldn't be found and who were knocked off course by relatively minor administrative hurdles (the electricity bill). These people had no faith in themselves and therefore – without necessarily wanting to do us harm – couldn't have much faith in our abilities. Every time we faced an exam, they got more alarmed than we did. They always asked multiple times if we had enough to wear when we went outside. They worried about our friends and our teachers. They were sure the holiday was going to turn into a disaster. Now these voices have become our own and cloud our capacity to take an accurate measure of what we are capable of and to teach others to achieve. We have internalised voices of irrational fear and fragility.

We need an alternative voice that can pause our runaway fears and remind us of the strengths we have latent within us, which the currents of panic have hidden from us. Our heads are large, cavernous spaces; they contain the voices of all the people we have ever known. We should learn to mute the unhelpful ones and focus on the voices we really need to guide us through the thickets. Knowing one is loved whatever happens to one in the world sets up ideal preconditions for doing well. It gives one the energy to take risks and feel resilient – without letting acute anxiety get in the way of performance.

Some of the most agitating moments in life are in essence failed teaching moments. To grasp this is to discover grounds for hope. Because – however unfamiliar the role of being a teacher might be to us – in plenty of areas outside a classroom there are opportunities to teach and to accept teaching as a learnable skill, at which it's perfectly reasonable to think one could get a little bit better.

## iii. In Defence of Politeness

It would be odd to be dead set against good manners. But, at the same time, our culture generally adopts an attitude of suspicion towards any conspicuous show of politeness. The idea of being 'well mannered' implies keeping certain aspects of the self carefully under wraps. It means deliberately controlling one's words, face and outward shows of emotion. In the Romantic era, many people became acutely aware of the potential negatives around manners. The philosopher Jean-Jacques Rousseau, in particular, saw manners as a kind of corruption. He hated the way in which politeness could enable a person to disguise their selfish, ruthless intentions behind a sleek and smiling exterior. By nature, he felt, an aggressive intention should be accompanied by a grimace and a snarl – and then you'd know what the other person was up to. And seeking to be polite and courteous came to be regarded as an affront to the authentic self. Politeness requires you to thank people you are not grateful to; to hypocritically compliment people you don't respect; to disown your true opinions and to sell your individuality to gain respectability. These are extreme attitudes, but some of the doubts linger. And so, today, the terms 'plainspoken' and 'forthright' carry a tinge of admiration.

The Romantic worries were focused on painful moments when the authentic self might be sidelined by oppressive social conventions or by a tyrannical insistence on being polite, whatever the cost – and by the opportunities afforded to the outwardly polished but inwardly malevolent character. But it's possible to acknowledge that there are certainly dangers attached to the idea of politeness while thinking that there's also quite a lot of useful work that manners can still do.

Is there any help to be found in the ideas of politeness and good manners when it comes to keeping a bit calmer around other people? Staying calm around others isn't the pursuit of icy indifference – wishing to remain unruffled and unbothered by them and their lives. The problem is that the degree of agitation and upset one is liable to feel gets in the way of doing the things we realise we should and ideally want to do. Getting upset and bothered too easily mucks up our relationships with other people.

To get a sense of what manners are for, it's worth revisiting the Romantic assumption that our natural instincts tend to be good and wholesome – which would make the artificial habits we call manners either pointless or even a bit sinister. It's an attractive idea, in the abstract. But unfortunately one of our settled instincts is to suppose that rage is a way of making things better. If you feel insulted, neglected or in any way threatened, instinct prompts that you should bare your teeth and make a big noise; the blood pumps faster, the nostrils flare. Or, at least, that you do things like call someone a piece of shit, troll them, slam a door, storm out, threaten legal action. Theoretically we see that this is nonsense. Getting furious actually – almost invariably – makes things much worse. But our grip on this insight is tragically weak.

Being polite and well mannered means – among other things – observing certain conventions. For instance, that it's not OK to shout in a restaurant, pretty much no matter what has happened. That you should not get visibly angry with anyone who is serving you. These rules assume that you feel like letting off steam, that you are getting worked up – and they deliberately insist you don't act on that feeling. The point of a code of politeness and of ideas of having good manners is to construct a barrier between having an emotion and expressing it. Instead of saying: 'I think that's a totally stupid idea', you feel the same thing, but you say: 'It's interesting you feel that way, but I wonder if that is necessarily the best strategy here. Perhaps you could say a little more about it.'

Politeness does not prevent a person from feeling angry or upset or hurt. What it does is delay the expression of the feeling. Manners counteract the rush to judgement. They allow a few moments for more information to emerge, for the ire to reduce slightly before doing anything decisive. The delay built into politeness allows you time to determine the true facts. It provides space to understand the issue behind the anger. If you knew more, you might not be so irate.

A major portion of flying off the handle is being premature. If one had better understood what was really going on, what the other person's intention was, what they thought we thought – if we grasped a little more the tangled background of misunderstandings, then we wouldn't feel quite so angry and desperate. It might be that if you could take time to work out what's actually going on in your mind, you'd discover that behind the anger is a feeling of shame at your own vulnerability; or that behind the impatience is a fear of failure. So politeness doesn't so much deny what one is genuinely feeling as provide a greater opportunity to discover one's emotions more accurately.

Politeness provides a way in which you can back down with dignity. In nature there is only ever one reason you cede the high ground – you are acknowledging defeat. You are bowing before a superior power. But under the rules of politeness, you let the other person off not because you are a weakling, a coward or a failure, but because you value calm over chaos. Politeness makes it easier to apologise, because apologising isn't just an act of pure submission.

Politeness is founded on a major insight into human nature and a big positive thesis about what civilisation is and why we need it. It's a view that was advanced particularly by the political philosopher Thomas Hobbes in the 17th century. Hobbes was acutely conscious that our normal, unrestrained instincts are far from being wholly nice. We may be quite inclined by nature to damage or destroy our rivals; to take advantage of those who are weaker than us; to grab more than our fair share of anything good if we can; to humiliate those who we feel are in some way alien; to revenge ourselves on anyone we feel has upset or disappointed us and to enforce our opinions and beliefs on others if we can. These are natural inclinations, Hobbes argues; therefore, we positively require a set of constraining conventions that artificially induce better ways of dealing with other people. Politeness is not mere decoration. It is directed at dealing with a major human problem: we need manners to restrain the beast inside.

## iv. On Bureaucracy

We grow up at the centre of a responsive world. Parents massively reorganise their lives so as to accommodate the needs of a new baby. They spend ages selecting just the right presents at birthdays and Christmas and blame themselves if the gifts fail to delight. Account is taken of a child's mood and physical state: if they're tired, we'll go home; if they're hungry, we'll eat. One of the ambiguous achievements of good parenting is that the child comes to assume that other people really can be alert to their needs. It's not always that we'll get just what we want, but that our genuine needs, properly stated, will meet with recognition and understanding.

But inevitably we will often run up against the rigid indifference of the wider world. A parking ticket won't be waived because you are in a hurry and need to pop into the corner shop to buy a lemon for stuffing the chicken for dinner. The tax office won't say, we understand, you've been a bit stressed recently and so why don't you just return your details when you can, we know how it is if you've been arguing with your partner and it saps your energy for form-filling. Citing these kinds of needs and troubles makes perfect sense in intimate relationships. We're often quite good at making allowances for friends, family, neighbours – and of course for children. We can be flexible when we want. But these attitudes stop applying when we cross the boundary from personal dealings to the zone that could be broadly summed up as 'bureaucracy'.

Bureaucracy is a reliable, ever-fertile source of agitation in our lives. You're calling the phone company to change your payment plan. They want to know your online account number, which you've forgotten. But you do have your password, your address, your mother's maiden name and information about your first pet (a collie-kelpie cross called Pipi, with a love of chewing carpets). Unfortunately, this won't suffice. The service person doesn't doubt your identity; you both know it would be bizarre for an impostor to attempt to use your credit card to reduce the payment on your phone connection. If they'd stolen your card why would they be carefully saving a small amount of money each month, and they'd have to have stolen your phone as well and not bothered to change the number. It's maddening. But without the particular account number, you can't proceed. It doesn't matter what the operator wants, because if the number isn't entered, the system won't make the changes. Human sympathy doesn't count for much in the face of the purely technical demand for a string of digits.

It's maddening not just because it is time-consuming and inconvenient. It sets off fundamental alarm bells. It's bringing one into a situation where compassion, understanding and human connections don't have the power to solve problems. Where 'who you are' (i.e. a pretty decent, honest, well-meaning individual) doesn't matter.

Or you arrive at the airline check-in kiosk just a couple of minutes after the flight has officially closed. You know the flight hasn't started boarding; they haven't even called passengers to the gate. A friend who arrived ten minutes ago and is on the same flight is actually standing next to you. You've only got a small bit of hand luggage; the plane isn't full (your friend was offered a choice of seats). But you can't get a boarding pass, because there's a rule that says when the flight is closed, it's closed. You won't be able to get home in time to read your daughter a bedtime story.

The deeper stress – which gets added to the sheer inconvenience of having to wait for the next plane – is that the details of your needs count for nothing against the purely formal requirements of an administrative system. Something that's humanly crucial – the warmth of your family life – can carry no weight here; you can't plead about the lonely child or about how you've missed them; the machine (or the overburdened member of staff you pour out your troubles to) cannot put things right.

The evolution of bureaucracy hasn't been an accident. In a traditional society, power is personal – and the relationship to the people is intimate. The clan chief knows and is related to the governed. So the idea of being understood is always there as a hope (however it might have been frustrated in practice): there's the sense that if you sway this individual they can do what they think is fitting and appropriate; they can decide for themselves what to do. Or it could be hugely unfair – the opportunities for favouritism, nepotism and bribery are endless.

Bureaucracy, on the whole, is a necessary component of a good-enough society. This was the point articulated by the German sociologist Max Weber at the very end of the 19th century. Modern government and industry operate on a large scale. And they attain a higher degree of efficiency and fairness by instituting systematic processes and standard rules and by setting up 'correct' ways of doing things. Officials and employees are required to apply the rules in an impartial and accurate way. And standing back, we know why this is so. It is to avoid favouritism and to avoid complicated special pleading that would massively clog up the system. But this leads, of course, to a conflict with the specific contours of the individual case.

The apparent unresponsiveness is not brought about by a deliberate desire to ignore people's particular situations. It's an unfortunate but largely unavoidable by-product of good and reasonable intentions. One's specific needs are being ignored in the broad interests of fairness, reducing costs and keeping a big, complex undertaking going. We get agitated when we find ourselves at the intersection of our own particular needs and the average, usual case that the system is designed to be good at dealing with. It's not – as our panicked reactions sometimes suggest – that bureaucracy is out to get us or that those who manage it are soulless robots. The explanation is strangely banal. It's that the price of an overall drive to efficiency is that some small percentage of cases will become horribly entangled for what look like tiny reasons. And every so often we will find ourselves at just such a point.

The desperation we sometimes feel around bureaucracy is part of a larger fact about the hardness and indifference of the external world. At key points, your needs, no matter how worthy, get nowhere: a hotel won't put you up because you are really longing to visit the city or could really do with a few days on a lounger by a pool; you can't get moved to the front of the supermarket checkout queue because you are feeling bored; the shop won't give you a pair of trousers because they suit you perfectly; the restaurant won't feed you because you are hungry. Or no matter how urgent some bit of work might be, your laptop has trouble communicating with the printer – you just get the message 'cannot locate printer'. And nothing you do seems to make any difference. Our private concerns – however intense and reasonable and good – on their own count for nothing in the face of the impersonal forces of commerce, technology and nature. We won't be cut any slack.

The calming move sees such unfortunate incidents as inevitable, rather than as avoidable affronts. They are unavoidable in the way that in the past the journey from Edinburgh to London could not be accomplished in less than a week, no matter how urgent the mission. A certain vision of the world made that time frame seem not shocking or disappointing or maddening, but completely necessary. One's irritation and hope would be focused on the margins: one might fervently hope to arrive in 167 hours and start to get very edgy if after 171 hours one was still somewhere in East Anglia. If we assume from the start that quite often technology will be baffling (because it is still in some respects in its own stagecoach era) then its failures are less offensive to us. If we take it for granted that banks, utility companies, airlines and governments will be significantly inefficient 5 per cent of the time, we will understand that every so often our dealings with them will get tangled. The foundation of such calm is understanding. Our wider understanding of the world and of history frames our sense of what is likely to happen and why. We move from irritating explanations – the company doesn't care, tech people are idiots – to less inflammatory and more accurate ones: the pursuit of efficiency will inevitably produce a certain number of maddening cases that don't fit the rule; the development of new technology will, inevitably, fall short of its most impressive versions in a significant number of ways.

Being calm does not mean one thinks the situation is nice or agreeable or interesting. It just means that one knows one is adding to the difficulties by fuming and seething to no good effect. Which, stated in the abstract, sounds like a very small development. But, when we recall the times of soul-churning rage, this reveals itself as a huge, and deeply benign, achievement.

Chapter Three:

# Work

## i. Capitalism

We deserve a great deal of sympathy for the fact that we are living under capitalism. In terms of human experience, it's a new and very complicated way of organising life. Economists define capitalism in quite technical ways: it means competition between firms for access to investment funds; it means demand is highly mobile, with customers switching from one supplier to another in search of a better deal; capitalism involves a strenuous devotion to innovation, with a constant battle to provide the public with newer and better products at lower prices. In this way, capitalism has brought many good things into people's lives. It has created elegant, exciting cars; delicious sandwiches; charming hotels on remote islands; bright, kindly kindergartens. And – more troublingly – some very anxious citizens.

The essential drive of capitalism is to provide more appealing goods at lower prices. While this is attractive for the customer, it is rather hellish for the producer: which of course means pretty much everyone in some major portion of their lives. The more productive an economy, the more conditions of employment will be less secure, less serene and more agitated than one might ideally like.

Capitalism has major psychological consequences. In the middle of the 19th century, Karl Marx summed up this aspect with a famous phrase, declaring that, in capitalism: 'All that is solid melts into air'. What he had in mind was that previous societies had been, on the whole, much more stable. They might have been poorer, but they were also in crucial ways more liveable. In a small town, the main streets might stay more or less the same for a hundred years; occasionally a wooden-frame house would be replaced with a stone one; a few trees might be cleared, a new barn erected; but from generation to generation the pattern of life would be strongly recognisable. But, during the 19th century, things started to change dramatically. Huge factories would spring up; there would be vast new housing developments; a railway would transform the economy of a town in a few years; jobs that hadn't existed would quickly emerge as massive areas of employment; new classes of people would become powerful, only to be displaced by others. People began to dream of past tranquillity and they were not merely being nostalgic.

In more contemporary detail, what capitalism means, in terms of day-to-day experience, is that your sense of your worth as a human being, and your basic sense of what your life is about, will – almost inevitably – become interwoven with how you are doing in your career. One is haunted by the thought: if only I were smarter, more hard-working, then I would achieve more, get larger payments and live a more satisfying life. The line of thought is tantalising because the rewards are continually dangled before one's eyes. The more comfortable airline seat, the beautiful kitchen units, the happy outings with the family, the feeling of being respected by one's peers. But these good things are only there if you strive and compete successfully. There is no reassuring guarantee that would allow you to truly relax.

The prospect of failure is always in the wings too. And the fall will be all the more painful and bitter because the meritocratic voice of the competitive economy will deliver the harsh message: outcomes are dependent on you; if you fail it's mainly your own fault. It's presented as a verdict on your character.

The economic conditions we sum up as capitalism will create agonising tensions between the demands of home life and the requirements of working life. A sudden shift in a crucial deadline will mean you have to work late just when you were hoping for a quiet time with your partner; you will end up being tired and cranky when you'd like to be warm and engaged. And at the same time you will be continually confronted by images of the very things you seek but are unable to accomplish in your own life – of families holding it together very well, of places where you can be relaxed and energetic and a good partner and glamorous all at the same time.

The harried feeling of being overbusy, and subject to too many demands, is not your own fault. It seems a bit odd to say, but our private agonies are tethered to big historical processes. Pains and troubles, which, seen close up, seem to have no explanation other than our own failings, deserve to be given a bigger context. History depersonalises the blame. It's not you: it's the stage of history you happen to be living through.

Depersonalising – and its accompanying passing of the responsibility onto the sweep of history – does not make the difficulty disappear. But the new, more accurate interpretation is a relief all the same. A parent who is struggling with a teenager who is becoming distant and critical might be hugely assisted by the concept of healthy separation. Instead of seeing their child's behaviour as a response simply to their own failings as a parent (which is the natural response), there's a more accurate and less distressing idea available: they are going through a process that is inherently quite difficult for all involved but that isn't a reflection on the specific failings of any particular individual. It's still painful, but it is relieved of its desperate edge. And with less blame circulating, it is possible to try to manage the process with a little more grace.

By contemplating the forces of capitalism and their impact on our private lives, we are zooming out from the intimate experience to the big explanation. And this takes the burden of guilt to some important extent off our own shoulders. The point isn't to say that capitalism is particularly awful. The fact that work under capitalism is at times very demanding and stressful doesn't entail that it's not worth doing or that there's some nicer alternative just round the corner. We accept, for instance, that bringing up children is often stressful and demanding, but don't think that it is therefore not worth undertaking. It's just that we're a bit better at factoring in the scale of the challenge we're facing. Through no error of our own, or indeed of anyone, we are collectively living through the age of competition and insecurity around work. It's not entirely our fault if we often feel very stressed indeed.

## ii. Ambition

We tend, collectively, to have a pretty high regard for ambition. Few people relish the thought of being regarded as lacking in this quality. But for all its positive aspects, ambition is a deep driver of agitation and distress in life. It might come in the guise of a worry about not knowing what to do with one's life. Other people seem to be finding their feet and setting out on a definite course, but you're left feeling you want to do something, but what? Nothing seems quite right. Or there might be a brooding anxiety – perhaps on a Sunday evening – about plotting the next career step. What's the right move? Where are the dangers? What area would it make most sense to push forward in? Is it time to change companies, set up on one's own? Or is this the moment to shift direction and get established in a new field?

Concerns with career are about money, of course. But they are also about something else: the ambition to make the best use of our talents and make a contribution to the lives of others. The drive to 'become who one is supposed to be' is the sort of thing that keeps people awake at night. We feel we harbour latent potential within us and the ideal career is the story of how that inner potential gets externalised in the most fruitful ways.

We're haunted by the ghosts of our potential: the uneasy parts of ourselves that can't find rest and make their presence felt at 3.00am, or driving down the motorway or when staring into the bathroom mirror. There's a painful gap between what we are actually doing and what we sense we are capable of, and all the time we're running out of days and speeding towards death. What we decide to do around career is the most fateful, consequential of decisions: with powerful implications for the kind of life we end up leading, for the way we will spend our too-brief existence on earth. These are stomach-churning thoughts. And, to make things worse, we feel that we ought not to have them.

The modern idea of a working life is strangely devoted to a pre-industrial vision of career decisions. It's a vision that derives from the Romantic ideal of vocation. In the Romantic era, the most socially esteemed thing to be was a poet or an artist. These were vocations, or callings. The process of becoming an artist or a poet wasn't really a choice. You didn't see yourself as making a rational selection between competing options. Something deep in your nature – your soul – was compelling you: this career was your natural destiny. You would know for sure that this was what you were meant to do. For a long time the highly-charged notion of a vocation was confined to only a very small range of activities. But it was gradually taken up more and more extensively. So that instead of a vocation being a rare and unusual thing to have, it became regarded as the normal way in which everyone would find work. Thanks to the notion of vocation, we find it easy to assume that there's an ideal kind of job for us – one that we are perfectly fitted for by nature and that will make us happy. The trouble then is to know what it is. The idea of a vocation suggests that the right job should announce itself to you; it should call out to you and grip your imagination. And if this isn't happening, maybe there's something wrong with you.

In order to face these troubles in a slightly calmer state of mind, we should admit the inherent dignity and complexity of the problem of working out what to do. This is what the idea of a vocation secretly undermines and downgrades. It says, yes, it really matters what you do, but the task of working out what to do isn't itself something you need to give much special attention to: you are supposed to know this instinctively. Follow your heart.

Rather than obey a Romantic-era faith in intuitive feeling, the process of working out what to do – or what to do next – should be recognised for what it is: one of the most tricky and complicated and tiring tasks we ever have to undertake. It should be normal to lavish intellectual attention on just this issue. It should be expected that we will, at points, require to seek a great deal of external help. At other points we might need to take a week away from everything and everyone and give ourselves over to solitary thinking, free from the pressures of pleasing (or deliberately confounding) anyone else.

Working out what to do takes all this effort and time not because we are stupid or self-indulgent, but because the decision builds on scattered and very imperfect bits of evidence. Confused shards of information are scattered across our experience. What are, in fact, one's strengths? There are moments of boredom, excitement, things we've coped well with, things that have been intriguing for a while and then neglected: all of these need to be located, decoded and interpreted and pieced together. We have to weigh up certain competing interests. How much risk is one capable of bearing without getting too stressed? How important is it to feel that other people normally feel quite a lot of respect for what you do? Finding accurate answers to these questions means building up a high level of self-knowledge. In an ideal culture there would be many novels that took this critical period of career direction thinking as their dramatic focus: with the central character emerging from their heroic journey of enquiry with a clear conviction

that they should go into events management or that this is the
time to shift direction and turn their longstanding interest in
avocados into a job.

One of the most poignant kinds of knowledge people develop
as they become writers is tolerance of the terrible first draft.
And of the second and third and maybe many, many more as
well. To someone starting out, it seems like a sign of incom-
petence to produce an initial version that lacks so many of
the qualities you'd expect to see in a polished piece of work.
There's an expectation that it should be relatively straightforward to string a few decent paragraphs together. The more
painful – but productive – insight is that it is actually very
tricky to do this. One's thoughts and associations all tumble
out of the mind in confused and disordered ways. The thing
you want to say is hidden behind a more familiar point. The
link between a couple of ideas isn't at all obvious. You can't tell
as yet what should come first and what fits in later. An author
might have to redraft the material ten or twenty times before
they can understand what it is they are actually trying to say.
This is simply how long it takes them to unjumble their ideas.
We're not all writing novels, of course, but the sequence of
drafts tells us something about the mind in general. There are
going to be long, tricky processes involving a lot of crossings
out, a lot of changes and repositioning of material as we try to
understand ourselves.

The big, consequential choices we try to make around career
and career development have to be made under inescapably adverse conditions. Often we are short of time, often we don't
know enough about the options. Ultimately we are attempting
to describe someone we can't possibly fully know: ourselves
at a future date, and guess as well as we can what will be best

for them. Circumstances will change; whole industries will rise and fall, but we will have built up certain sets of skills, acquired distinctive social connections, fitted ourselves for a future we are only imagining.

We are often exposed primarily to the people in the public realm who have been unusually good at externalising their talents and acting on their ambitions. By necessity we hear more of these people even though they are in fact pretty rare and – hence – not a reasonable or helpful base for comparison. We would benefit from hearing more about a different range of role models who reveal another, more standard pattern: they cling to mistaken assumptions, take wrong turnings, step carefully away from what later turns out to have been the best option, and commit themselves enthusiastically to disastrous courses of action.

The universal plight – pretty much – is a sad one. We will almost certainly die with much of our potential undeveloped. Much of what you could have done will remain unexplored. And you may well go to the grave with parts of yourself pleading for recognition, or carrying a sense of failure that there was so much you didn't manage to do. But this isn't really a cause for shame. It ought to be one of the most basic things we recognise about each other: a common fate we face. It's very sad. But it is not sad uniquely to any one person. It's a strangely consoling tragic idea that imagination always, inevitably, outstrips the potential. Everyone is unfulfilled, and that's just a consequence of the odd way our minds have evolved.

## iii. Patience

Theoretically, work is the part of life where things get done; we don't lounge around or daydream; ideas get put into action, progress is made, there are tangible results. And on a grand scale one can be deeply impressed by the collective achievement of human labour: work creates cities and airlines, it builds hospitals and schools, it creates global supply chains and brings astonishing innovations into existence. But when we zoom in and look at how things go day-to-day, it often looks horribly different. This morning, we need to discuss some data with the market research team, but the key person is away; there's a conference call to confirm the client is happy with the approach, but it emerges they can only give a provisional assent, and they need to have more time to check with all their stakeholders on the project (and even then it will turn out that someone is pushing for a few important revisions); then after eight rounds of discussion the main person who was supporting the venture moves to another role, and their successor has a different point of view; it turns out there are some tricky legal issues that need attention and the company tax implications are unclear; we're trying to get more support from a slightly sceptical partner. It can seem as if work is primarily an arena of exasperation and delay.

When he was trying to define what makes for good drama, the ancient Greek philosopher Aristotle concentrated on what makes a story maximally comprehensible: he thought that the story should unfold quickly in one place, with only a few clearly described main characters. The action shouldn't be very complicated; and everything should unfold in a logical way: there should be an obvious starting point, a decisive, definite ending and a direct route between the two in the middle. He was mapping out an ideal pace at which we'd like our working lives to unfold.

But in reality this is very far from how things usually go. The drama of our professional endeavours might have dozens or hundreds of characters in them, many of whom we don't really know, or whose motives we never properly understand. We can't quite tell when things are over. Maybe this is just a pause while people regroup? Maybe it is truly over? Maybe we are still really at the start of a bigger process? Or maybe we are heading in the wrong direction and actually getting further away from the hoped-for endpoint? Our minds naturally demand a clearer, more satisfying, pattern than is actually provided for by the messy processes of reality. And frustration, disappointment and impatience are some of the names we can give to divergence between the ideal model and the way things actually unfold.

One of the phrases that has been concocted in the attempt to instil a greater measure of patient endurance in the minds of the impetuous is the proverbial statement that Rome wasn't built in a day. It is intended to draw our attention to a stellar example of great but exceedingly slow achievement. According to tradition, it required almost exactly nine centuries for the city to evolve from the original settlement of clay huts to its grandest and most powerful metropolitan condition, under the Antonines, and particularly under the Stoic philosopher Marcus Aurelius, who was emperor from AD 161 to 180. There were many reversals and times of immense difficulty along the way: the city was sacked and besieged and burned; there were civil wars and riots and some terrible leaders. Nonetheless, below the very choppy surface, a long arc of development could clearly be traced. It was an arc that was hard for people to see at any particular moment, but could all the same clearly be recognised in retrospect.

By invoking this celebrated instance, we are trying to force upon ourselves a truth that in the abstract feels utterly obvious, but that – in fact – we find very hard to fully appreciate at the important moments when we really need it. We have to live day-to-day. But many worthwhile projects take years. We get frustrated at how little progress there appears to be. The seemingly minuscule rate of progress offends our need for speed and narrative cohesion; we long to feel that we are getting somewhere; we long to see solid results.

The statement isn't merely a call for patience; it's not just saying, 'Some things took a very long time to complete so what are you moaning about?' It is a reminder of what patience is grounded in: namely, an understanding of how certain processes really work. The phrase is pointing to a major cause of agitation: that we don't have a proper understanding of how long certain things are likely to take, and therefore we expect them to be accomplished more quickly and simply than is in fact reasonable.

One of the dispiriting thoughts when learning the piano or Italian is that one is making insufferably slow progress. We've got an image in our heads of rapid acquisition that is, in fact, unrealistic. We're not basing our expectations on a proper understanding of the process by which we actually get good at things (which, like the construction of Rome, follows an indirect route with many seeming detours and setbacks).

Reminding ourselves that building Rome took ages – and a lot of stress and frustration – counteracts an unfortunate side effect of a certain type of corporate and creative kindness, which is to conceal from the user the type of labour that went into creating the goods and services we enjoy. Businesses politely keep from us that the person who established the bottled water company, whose product one is now casually sipping, passed many nights of teeth-grinding, had tantrums, alienated her children, wept, and on one occasion threw up after a particularly frustrating meeting with a French plastics supplier. Because we tend much more to encounter the final result – after all the difficulties have been resolved – it's fatally easy to give ourselves an unduly streamlined, simplified and pleasant picture of how it all came about.

Impatience is not so much frustration at things taking a long time in any absolute sense, but the feeling that they are taking longer than they should. Sometimes this may truly be the case. But often the problem is not so much in the time 'things' take as in our assumptions about how long they are supposed to take. And we bring this tight time frame to bear primarily out of ignorance. It is because we don't fully understand the nature of a task that we do not budget accurately for how long it should take.

## iv. Colleagues

Through the 19th and 20th centuries, a new and powerful image of the ideal working environment started to emerge: the studio. It was often characterised by sloping ceilings, large windows, a view over the neighbouring rooftops, sparse furniture, the smell of turpentine, messy tables covered in tubes of paint and half-finished masterpieces propped against the walls. But there was one additional factor that particularly enticed the collective imagination: the studio was a place of solitude. There the artist would be alone – without interference or disturbance, able to carry out their own plans and projects without the need to ask anyone's permission or approval. From first to last they would have total control over their own work.

The studio continues to speak powerfully to the modern imagination – not just as a prestigious physical place, but as the location of an ideal. The factory and, especially, the office feel like places of compromise, frustration, mediocrity and interference by comparison with the Romantic ideal of the artist's studio. In the studio you can do it all yourself; you don't need colleagues. And therefore you're freed from one of the deep and rich sources of agitation in modern life: the need to collaborate and work alongside other people.

There's a painful ring of truth to the preference for the studio over the office. But we've not almost all ended up in offices because we have mysteriously failed to notice that we'd be doing much better if we could work alone. The rationale of teams and offices lies in the stubborn, unavoidable fact that a huge range of commercial and administrative tasks cannot be undertaken by individuals working mainly on their own. Sadly, you can't run an airline or operate an urban design practice on your own.

Many tasks can't be accomplished solo and therefore we face a whole range of problems and encounter one of the things that will – across an entire life – do more than almost anything else to rob our lives of calm: managers, co-workers and employees.

Our public story of work is dominated by solo artists. Glamour has accumulated around their lonely struggles and their individual achievements. Prestige and interest attach to the individual effort; we are much more likely to read an interview with a star than with a team of support staff. We take this for granted; we feel it's obvious that the experience of the star is more interesting. Our fantasy vision of what work is supposed to be like takes us away from a just appreciation and understanding of what we are most likely to face every day. We don't develop proper recognition for the skills and qualities of mind that in fact help make collaboration successful, productive and enjoyable.

The task of collaboration is, in fact, beautiful and serious. It is one of the grandest undertakings to coordinate the efforts of groups of people. In a few special cases we have learned to appreciate this: we admire the choir that can sing harmoniously and the orchestra that can collectively perform a symphony. Ideally we should recognise that similar skills of cooperation are required in less prestigious (but equally necessary) activities: the implementation and monitoring of risk management programmes to ensure continuity of supply in adverse scenarios for a supermarket chain.

The office requires a set of skills that are unnecessary in the studio, and at the back of our mind we resent having to acquire these techniques. Compromise, clear and simple explanation, listening carefully before making an objection, keeping one's ego under control, not taking offence where none was intended, learning to see what might be good about an idea that you didn't think of: these qualities have yet to attain the level of public esteem they in fact deserve. They don't entice our imaginations, and yet, they should. Because they can contribute to our lives as much as, or more than, the qualities we have come to associate with artists.

When we get angry, impatient, disappointed and generally maddened by those we work with, there is a fatally attractive explanation of our troubles always to hand: we are surrounded by unusually lax or incompetent people. But in fact it is – inescapably – difficult to work well with other people. And there are a few big, unavoidable reasons why that's the case.

The central problem of colleagues is that they are not you. To grasp why this matters so much, we need to contemplate the condition of the baby who does not realise that its mother is in fact a separate being. Only after a long and very difficult process of development (if ever) can a child realise that a parent is truly a distinct individual with an entire life and history outside their relationship to their child – and it may be the work of a lifetime to gradually accept that this is the case.

We largely persist in modelling our sense of what other people are like – and of what might be going on in their heads – on our experience of ourselves. We find it remarkably difficult to imagine clearly and calmly that others might not be very much like us at all. Others have different skills, different weaknesses, different motives and fears. It is as if the human brain did not evolve with the need to address this particular problem. And it may have been that for most of the time that human beings have existed it has been sufficient – for individual and group survival – to operate with a very limited interest in how people might differ from us in terms of how their minds work.

In the office, other people are out of our control – and yet we need their assistance in performing delicate, complicated tasks. When we are doing things ourselves, we don't actually give ourselves clear instructions. If we could listen in to the accompanying inner monologue as we undertake a project, it would be made up of (to anyone else) a baffling series of assertions and jumbled words: 'Narr, yes. Come on! Ah, nearly, nononono, back … OK got it got it … NO. Yes. That's fine.' This might be the inner set of instructions (accompanied by biting the lower lip and hunching slightly forward) for selecting identifying images to accompany a certain passage of text.

But when we collaborate, we have to learn to turn the stream of consciousness (which only we can follow) into instructions, suggestions, commands and prompts that will be clear and effective for other people. Others can't by instinct alone understand what you need: they don't share your vision and their interests are not aligned. It's an extremely difficult thing to transform our own inner convictions and attitudes and motives into material that makes sense to other people, and it's not our fault if we're not naturally good at it.

Collaboration is difficult, in addition, because everyone, beneath the surface, is quite weird, and hence it requires a lot of special abilities and development to actually get the best out of working alongside them. We get frustrated by collaboration not simply because it is difficult, but because it is much more difficult than we suppose it should be. Recognising the inner strangeness of others (and of oneself) provides an accurate basis for the assumption that, on the contrary, collaboration is obviously a very tricky thing to attempt; it is extremely likely to encounter a great many obstacles that will take plenty of time to resolve.

We need to continually feed our quickly depleted readiness to make allowances for other people, to accept that things that are easy for us are hard for them, that they need encouragement, that a blunt statement, however true, may have a catastrophic effect. We don't habitually make accommodation for the complicated psychologies, odd scars and unexpected areas of fearsome vulnerability that others will inevitably have – but rarely look as if they do. It may take a great deal of thought and attention to work out how to manage a colleague on a particular matter. But we won't invest this time and effort if we suppose that everyone is (and ought to be) straightforward. The calmer starting point is to assume that of course collaboration is very tricky, but that the task of working well with others is noble and interesting – it is deserving of much thought and care and the constant renewing of attempts to make it work in non-panicked moments.

Chapter Four:

# The Sources of Calm

## i. Sight

The route to calm can follow two paths: one we've been trac-
ing up to this point – philosophy – and another we'll turn
to now – art. Philosophy aims to calm us down by reaching
us through our rational faculties. Art is concerned with how
concepts can affect us through our senses. The arts know
that we are physical, sensuous creatures and that there will be
points when it is wiser to touch us viscerally than argue with
us intellectually.

The Ryōan-ji Temple Zen garden is a major tourist attraction on
the northern fringes of Kyoto in Japan. Visitors go there to sit
on a wooden terrace and look for a long time at a patch of gravel that has been raked into lines and at some rocks surrounded
by clumps of moss. To people accustomed to Western tourist
destinations, it can feel like a very odd place. The gravel and the
rocks don't seem to 'mean' anything. They don't commemorate
a significant event or have any supernatural associations. Instead, the purpose of coming here is nothing more than to gain
a profound sense of calm. The visitor stands to learn how to
lead a more serene life from the visual experience of attending
to a carefully tended garden of pebbles, rocks and moss.

Top: Ryōan-ji Temple Zen rock garden in the spring, Kyoto, Japan
Bottom: Buddha stone figure, Bali

The garden is guided by a single simple idea: that what is presented externally to our senses can have a powerful impact on what happens to us internally, in our thoughts and emotions. The mind, in other words, can be guided by the senses. It's an idea that has traditionally offended clever people – because it bypasses the centres of cognitive intelligence and violates the idea that the mind is primarily influenced by information and arguments. The garden resolutely doesn't offer any facts or theories. It doesn't wrestle intellectually with us; it simply presents our eyes with a very precisely organised sensory experience.

The same idea – that sensory experience can shape our feelings – is at work in other parts of Buddhism. For centuries, devotees have been making statues of the Buddha himself. He's generally shown with his legs crossed; his eyes are closed in gentle concentration and he is ever so slightly smiling. He seems profoundly at peace with himself. The point of contemplating the Buddha is disarmingly simple: we should learn to *be* as he *looks*. We should model our inner world on his representation, searching for our own version of his comfortable, generous serenity.

The Western tradition asks us to concentrate on the Buddha's ideas. Buddhism more wisely remembers that we are sometimes as influenced by someone's smile. The faces of those we surround ourselves with start to shape our inner landscapes. Psychoanalysts speak of the way a mother's smile transmits contentment to a child – who absorbs the message and smiles back. Moods are contagious. By regularly looking carefully at the Buddha's tranquil, self-contained face, we boost a set of desirable qualities in ourselves; we promote our own always-endangered reserves of calmness and tranquillity.

The ambition to create deliberately calming environments hasn't been confined to Buddhism. It was also a powerful force within medieval Christian architecture. The Abbey of Cîteaux, not far from Dijon, was built by Cistercian monks during the 12th century. When the monks first arrived, the surrounding area was marshland and wilderness, but they soon developed it into a significant centre of industrial enterprise. They were involved in land reclamation, construction, agriculture, metallurgy, viniculture, brewing and education. They also strongly believed that this intense activity should be undertaken in an atmosphere of order and calm. They wanted to approach their labours in the best state of mind. Calm was their guiding psychological, and therefore also architectural, principle.

The Cistercian monks constructed simple and harmonious buildings out of the local limestone, with plain colours and few ornaments. The plans involved regular repetitions: the doors, windows and roof vaults wouldn't vary much, so that the eye would easily find points of reference. Everything felt solid and enduring. Our natural human frailty was to contrast with the immemorial tone of the masonry. The monks were particularly keen on cloisters: covered walkways opening onto a quiet central square around which one could take de-stressing walks even on a rainy afternoon. The abbey at Cîteaux was just one of thousands built with similar intentions over a period of hundreds of years. It's not an accident that architecture that sets out to create a contemplative and serene atmosphere can easily get labelled 'monastic', though in truth there's nothing inherently religious or Christian about the pursuit of calm. The longing for serenity is a continuing, widespread human need, although the overtly religious background to abbeys and monasteries has an unfortunate association: making calm places erroneously seem as if they were inherently connected to a belief in Jesus.

Monks' dormitory in Santa Maria Monastery, Ribatejo Province, Portugal

We need to rediscover the search for calm as a fundamental ambition of all architecture, not least for the buildings of our own harried times.

Artists have over the centuries also taken the development of calm to be at the centre of their mission to the world. In the 17th century, the French painter Claude Lorrain specialised in depicting soft skies, still water and stately, gentle trees. One of his famous techniques is to lead the eye gradually deeper and deeper into the silvery distance, towards the receding ridges of hills – drawing us into a much calmer world than the one we normally inhabit. Claude was trying to create a visual scene that would pacify our emotions, so that our minds could become (for a little while) as subdued and harmonious as his landscapes. He was working within the Classical assumption that painting – like all the arts – should help us to develop our souls, and since staying calm is a major concern in life, he accepted that calm would be one of the big goals that any really ambitious artist would set themselves.

This way of thinking about art has, however, got sidelined by a more recent, Romantic tendency to think of art as existing 'for art's sake' – which feels awkward around identifying any very clear or direct way in which works of art might be useful to us. The whole notion of art being in some way therapeutic came to seem unsophisticated. So, even when modern works of visual art actually are strategic instruments for calming us down, we might be slow to take up the offer.

The 20th-century American artist Agnes Martin, for instance, was deeply interested in calming manoeuvres. When asked by an interviewer to explain the purpose of her paintings, with their studied abstractness and repeated pale grids, she remarked that contemporary life agitates us like never before, so that time spent with her work should hopefully 'take our minds in another direction'. Though the commentary of museums and learned guides seldom puts matters as simply or as usefully, Martin was offering – via her grids and neat lines – the same form of help as Claude via his horizons and radiant clouds, as the monks of Ryōan-ji via their moss and rocks and as the sculptors of the Buddha via the quiet smile of their philosophical sage. In all cases, we are being offered a representation of an outer form that should incite and bolster an inner disposition.

At certain moments, it can feel obvious that externals matter for mood. One looks in a tidy cupboard and feels a glow of serene satisfaction. An early-evening walk in a park or by the beach can be deeply consoling. We're very alive in a few

Claude Lorrain, *Landscape with Hagar and the Angel*, 1646

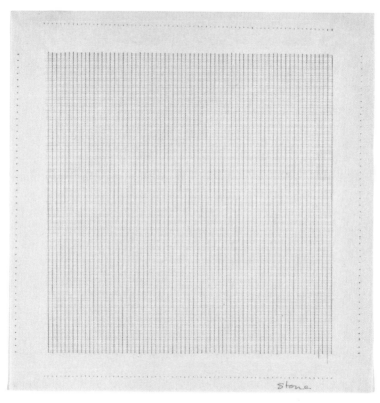

Agnes Martin, *Stone*, 1964

personal moments to the impact of what we see. But often this attitude isn't one we are strongly and securely committed to. The thought that mood is affected by the visual environment is a blow to our rational self-respect and our sense of being reasonably robust individuals. We're reluctant to say that we might suffer from visual chaos. It can easily come across as unduly fussy or a touch pretentious. That's why, at a political level, the pursuit of calm design, in cities or the countryside, is never a priority. The idea that our mental health depends on serene environments has got very little traction: that's why we have a lot of bright neon signs and ugly towers all around us.

In the West, this very issue – how much visual externals really matter – was at the heart of one of the biggest disputes in the history of ideas, with the two great religious traditions – Catholicism and Protestantism – lined up on opposing sides.

The very first church building put up specifically for Protestant worship was the Castle Chapel in Torgau (two hours' drive south from Berlin), consecrated by Martin Luther in 1544. The design was deliberately severe and functional; it was simply a space to keep out the rain and the cold, where you could pray and think and hear sermons. You were supposed to be influenced only by ideas. Anything else – paintings, statues and beauty in general – were seen as snares that would seduce the congregation away from what really mattered. This was diametrically opposed to the Catholic view. The Catholic Frari church in Venice – for instance – contains a large number of hugely complex and expensive paintings and pieces of sculpture. It was intended to be a sensorily alluring place. It was somewhere people would like to spend time, even if they weren't feeling especially pious that day. The construction and decoration of this building were guided by a strong conviction

Top: Interior view of the Castle Chapel in Torgau, Saxony, Germany
Bottom: Nave of the Santa Maria Gloriosa dei Frari church, Venice, Italy

that you could use the visual environment to get people into the right mood – so that they would be more receptive to ideas. The Catholic view grows from the notion that we are hybrid creatures, sensuous as much as we are spiritual. Inner life is hugely dependent on externals, so we should be very careful and ambitious about organising external space so as best to serve our inner needs. That's why the Catholic Church in its most impressive periods invested so deeply in creating the finest buildings and art in the world at the time. These were not created for their own sake but as concerted, systematic attempts to elevate the soul of humanity.

The same debate over the role of visuals rumbles on into modern times – though shorn of any references to religion. The neo-Protestant view repudiates any ties between the inner and the outer realms: it suggests that it doesn't matter what clothes a person wears, what houses look like, what the visual character of a city is. These are dismissed as unimportant subjects, which don't need or even deserve any collective concern. There's a suspicion of any stress on externals, which are viewed in an unflattering light, as an unpleasant kind of showing off and status-seeking. But opposed to this, we find a neo-Catholic approach that holds that there are indeed intimate and deep reasons to care about what things look like: that we need to have the right sort of streets, train stations, libraries, kitchens and clothes in order to be the right sort of people. Independent of any religious preoccupation, modern secular neo-Catholics continue to see visual art and design as important routes to inner contentment.

It is, in a sense, tempting to side with the neo-Protestant view. It makes us less vulnerable to what is around us, to the colour of the walls, the design of the city or the quality of the hotel room. Most of what we see around us is haphazard and jumbled, an enemy of calm and concentration. Yet it may be truer to accept that, however complicated and humbling it can be, the visual atmosphere we move in does play a critical role in forming our moods. It isn't foolish to seek calm through our books, our ideas and our conversations; but alongside such moves, we should not be insulted also to be directed towards a more basic set of manoeuvres: ensuring that our cupboards are tidy, our beds made, our walls hung with quiet scenes and our gardens well raked. We need to lay our harassed eyes on calming art as much as we need to bathe our minds with calming logic.

## ii. Sound

One of the most calming things that societies have ever devised is the lullaby. In almost every culture there has ever been, mothers have rocked and sung their babies to sleep. It's clear that sounds can have a deeply soothing effect on us. We recognise the same phenomenon when we find it comforting to hear the sounds of waves on the shore, or leaves rustling in a breeze.

The general idea that sounds can influence our state of mind isn't itself controversial. But we don't, however, usually put it to systematic, ambitious use: as a tool to manage our emotions and powerfully target our most agitated states.

A humbling point that a lullaby reveals is that it's not necessarily the words of a song that make us feel more tranquil. The baby doesn't understand what's being sung but the sound has its effect all the same. The baby is showing us that we are all tonal creatures – responsive to the character of sounds – long before we are creatures of understanding who can decode the meaning of words. We operate on more than one level of communication and the musical may be the primary and most effective one at times. As adults, we are of course more familiar with semantic communication: we grasp the significance of the words, phrases and sentences another person uses. But there's a sensory level, in which the tone, rhythm and pitch of the sounds we hear affects us far more than anything another could possibly tell us. The musician can, at points, trump anything the philosopher might express.

Ancient Greek mythology was fascinated by the story of the famous musician Orpheus. At one point he had to rescue his wife from the underworld. To get there he needed to make his

way past Cerberus, the ferocious three-headed dog who guarded the entrance to the land of the dead. Orpheus was said to
have played such sweet, enchanting music that the wild beast
calmed down and became – for a while – mild and docile. The
Greeks were giving themselves a reminder of the psychological power of music. Orpheus didn't reason with Cerberus, he
didn't try to explain how important it was that he should be
allowed to pass, he didn't speak about how much he loved his
wife and how much he wanted her back. Cerberus was – as
we ourselves are at times of distress – pretty much immune to
reason. But he was still open to influence. It was a matter of
finding the right channel to reach him.

When we feel anxious or upset, kindly people sometimes try
to comfort us at the semantic level by pointing to facts and
ideas: they try to influence our thinking and – via careful arguments – to quieten our distress. But, as with Cerberus, the
more effective way to deal with the problem might at points be
to soothe us via the senses. We might need to be quietened and
made mild (by a lullaby or a Chopin prelude) before we are in
any position to listen to reason.

There is a long history of linking particular chords and keys to
specific areas of emotional experience; the German poet and
theorist Christian Daniel Friedrich Schubart associated the key
of G major – for instance – with 'calm and satisfied passion
… tender gratitude … every gentle and peaceful emotion of
the heart'. These are pretty good generalisations and they support the idea that the power of certain pieces of music to calm
us down is not, at heart, mysterious. In contact with certain
pieces of music, our hearts – musical boxes of their own – start
to follow the slower rhythms of voices and instruments; guided
by the music, one's breathing grows more even and placid. We

don't have to be persuaded of anything: the effects occur at a physical level first and they in turn influence the character of our thoughts.

What this means is that – in principle – we can set out to create music that deliberately targets emotional needs, in a way that's not entirely different from the attempts by medical researchers to create drugs that effectively address psychological ailments. This isn't currently a highly esteemed creative task. But that's not always been so. When the world's greatest musical talents worked to a religious agenda, composers often set out to quite deliberately work the listener into a particular frame of mind. And often the ambition was to create a sense of inner peace. For instance, in hearing Schubert's 'Ave Maria' (composed in 1825), one feels enfolded in a generous, tender embrace; one will encounter no criticism or rebuke but endless depths of understanding and compassion for one's troubles. The music lifts us up and gently distracts us from the immediate cause of agitation (as a parent might try to distract an upset child).

Peter Gabriel's 'Don't Give Up' is designed as a similar kind of musical therapy. It's intended to be taken at points where we feel like giving up, when we've lost all confidence and feel crushed by the demands of the world. The strategy is to be as sympathetic as an imagined mother: first to acknowledge the horribly painful sense of failure and then to offer a kindly reassurance. The message is not that one's plans will inevitably work out, but that one's human worth is not on the line if they don't. The music offers us what at such points we can't offer ourselves: compassion and faith.

Yet these musical creations are closer to exceptions than they should be. Culturally, we have not fully seized on the opportunities for calm offered us by music. We've come to think that music shouldn't have a deliberate, purposeful intent. It shouldn't set out to make a specific, beneficial intervention in one's emotional life. We are readier to reach for a drug than a song.

In a wiser, more ambitious arrangement of society, we would have music trials akin to medical trials, with acoustic laboratories making slight adjustments to all the elements of a piece of music – the rhythm, tonal range, melodic line, timbre and pitch of the sounds – and assessing the difference this makes to those who listen to it. We would be building up knowledge of what aural interventions could work in relation to which species of agitation. We would determine that some people might have an adverse reaction to a chord of A minor and that a flute would, for example, be especially relevant to tensions around sexual fantasy within marriages.

The idea of using sound to affect moods was most ambitiously practised by Christian churches, who were keen to recruit the talents of the most impressive composers of their times. In the 1730s and 1740s, for example, J. S. Bach produced his Mass in B minor. Particular pieces were written to stimulate appropriate emotions for each part of the religious ceremony. For instance, near the beginning there is the Kyrie: a call to the congregation to recognise the ways they've hurt and wronged others, and a plea that God will forgive their unkindness. Here the music is very sombre, with a five-voice fugue theme (alto, soprano I, soprano II, tenor, bass) and a stepwise ascending melody, interrupted by a lower sighing motif, encouraging us to feel repentance about our own failings while hinting at the possibility of redemption. Later there is the Credo: the assertion of religious faith, for which the music is more confident and majestic, advancing in a polyphonic formation, with a sequence of fugue entries. The ambition was to help people get into the right frame of mind to best engage with each section of the religious service. Bach recognised that one might need encouragement to feel sorry or to feel confident. He was highly realistic about our normal tendency to get distracted, to start thinking about stray and random details even at quite important moments, and he used every aspect of his musical genius to keep us trained on what he believed to be quite literally the most important ideas in the universe.

The Christian religion also got very interested in the musical potential of pipe organs – which were very widely installed in churches. In particular, it was the potential of the very low notes that organs could reach that was of interest. As the congregation entered the church, the organ would play a sequence of deep, harmonic rumbles, sometimes including notes too low to be perceived by the ear but having a physical effect all the same. These profound tremors would reliably influence the sentiments: making people feel a sense of awe, humility and calm.

The modern age can be rather negative about these efforts. They can be seen as manipulative and as attempts to 'brainwash' audiences. But one doesn't have to agree with the particular messages they were promoting in order to see the value of the psychological resource they were systematically tapping into. We can share the underlying conviction that music and sound can and should be used in highly organised ways to help us contain and direct our feelings in ways that improve our lives – even though we might have a different idea of what improving our lives might look like.

If we were more ambitious and systematic about using the potential of sound to improve our emotional lives, and in particular to calm ourselves down, we'd go carefully through our days, identifying trigger points of agitation – and creating playlists in response. The early morning might be a particularly appropriate moment to hear the sounds of the *ngoni*, a traditional lute found throughout West Africa, with a reassuring big sound, like that of a comforting father, and made of a hollowed-out, canoe-shaped piece of wood with dried animal skin stretched over it like a drum. This might be a moment where a dose of something very cheerful and energetic would work. In the minutes before we sit down to a family dinner, it might be that the effective intervention would be something rousing and heartening – like the songs people sang before going into battle – or perhaps the useful thing would be music that suggested an eternal perspective, like a Handel choral movement, which would boost one's immune system around petty irritants.

We know that in certain moods we are better able to apologise – and thus quieten a distracting conflict – or to be calmly assertive about our needs, and hence avoid building up resentment; or we are more easily able to brush off a setback or more comfortable with disagreement, or more willing to take a back seat and let someone else make the running. Finding the music that helps us enter these beneficial states of mind is a serious and hugely constructive task. We've tended to underplay it because we've been slow to recognise just how big the impact of mood on our lives really is, and hence how crucial the wise management of mood must always be.

## iii. Space

Sometimes we respond quite negatively to encounters with things that are much larger and more powerful than ourselves. It's a feeling that can strike us when we are alone in a new city, trying to negotiate a vast railway terminal or the huge underground system at rush hour, and we sense that no one knows anything about us or cares in the least for our confusions. The scale of the place forces upon us the unwelcome fact that we don't matter very much in the greater scheme and that the things that are of great concern to us don't figure much at all in the minds of others. It's a potentially crushing, lonely experience that intensifies anxiety and agitation.

But there's another way an encounter with the large scale can affect us – and calm us down.

Heading back to the airport after a series of frustrating meetings, the sunset behind the mountains is magnificent: tiers of clouds are bathed in gold and purple, huge slanting beams of light cut across the urban landscape. To record the feeling without implying anything mystical, it seems as if one's attention is being drawn up into the radiant gap between the clouds and the hills, and that one is for a moment merging with the cosmos. Normally the sky isn't a major focus of attention, but now it's mesmerising. For a while it doesn't seem to matter so much what happened in the meeting or the fact that the contract will – maddeningly – have to be renegotiated by the Paris team. It's strangely calming and comforting to be absorbed in the contemplation of something vastly bigger than oneself.

Artists and philosophers have given this feeling a name: the Sublime. We experience this sensation of the Sublime whenever we are hugely impressed by something that seems much larger and more powerful than we are. It overwhelms us with its grandeur while also offering us a vivid sense of our own relative littleness. At this moment, nature seems to be sending us a humbling message: the incidents of our lives are not terribly important in the scheme of things. And yet, strangely, rather than being distressing, this sensation can be immensely comforting and calming.

The Sublime is calming because it counteracts a persistent and very normal source of distress in our lives. Our minds naturally focus on what is immediately before us. We instinctively get deeply engaged with whatever happens to be close to us in space and time. And we have a proportionally less intense, more detached relationship to things that feel very far off. It's not a surprising arrangement. Very often, what's immediately present is more relevant to our survival than what happened five years ago or might happen much later in our lives. Our minds are geared to fleeing a snake or staving off hunger. Translated into the terms of modern life, it means that last night's squabble over flecks of toothpaste on the bathroom mirror and the work deadline of Tuesday morning feel hugely agitating – though in terms of the overall meaning of a relationship, career or of a whole life, they are in fact pretty minor incidents. The problem is, our minds are structured so as to give maximum attention to what is happening now – whereas, to actually see the importance of anything we have to situate it in a much larger frame of reference.

What the Sublime does is – very unusually – to foreground our engagement with the larger horizons of existence. Instead of looking at this or that detail (which therefore seems very big, because it dominates the current moment), we've got an experience in which the specifics of our lives are seen as proportionally much smaller and therefore as posing a far less significant threat to us. Things that have up to now been looming large in our minds (what's gone wrong with the Singapore office, the fact that a colleague behaved coldly, the disagreement about patio furniture) tend to get cut down in size. The Sublime drags us away from the minor details that normally – and inevitably – occupy our attention and makes us concentrate on what is truly major. Local, immediate irritants are reduced, for a while, in their power to bother us.

The painful comparison of our own situation with that of others whom we feel are more fortunate is an unhappily reliable source of psychological distress. It tends to make us feel irritated with ourselves – if only we pushed ourselves harder, didn't make so many blunders and could overcome our laziness, we'd perhaps be able to raise ourselves to their level. Or we get more and more annoyed by the external obstacles that seem to stand in our way. The encounter with the Sublime is helpful here too because it doesn't just make oneself look comparatively small. It undercuts the gradations of human status and makes them – at least for a time – look relatively fairly unimpressive too. Next to the canyon or ocean, even the king or the CEO does not seem so mighty.

The sight of the dry expanses of a desert offer a philosophy of calm embodied in matter: the way it suggests that year by year little will change; a few more stones will crumble from the mesa; a few plants will eke out an existence; the same pattern of light and shadow will be endlessly repeated. There is a stark separation from human concerns and priorities. And this separation applies to everyone equally. The spaces of the desert are indifferent not to me in particular but to humanity in general. Caring about having a larger office or being worried that one's car has a small scratch over the left rear wheel or that the sofa is looking a bit moth-eaten doesn't make much sense against a vastness of time and space. The differences in accomplishments, standing and possessions between people don't feel especially exciting or impressive when considered from the emotional state that the desert promotes. The desert seems to be trying to convince us of a number of things that usefully correct and balance out our standard ways of thinking. Here, little things seem hardly worth getting bothered or upset about. There's no urgency. Things happen on the scale of centuries. Today and tomorrow are essentially the same. Your existence is a small temporary thing. You will die and it will be as if you had never been.

It could sound demeaning. But these are generous sentiments, for we otherwise so easily exaggerate our own importance and suffer accordingly. We are truly minute and entirely dispensable. The world would trundle on much the same without us. The Sublime does not humble us by exalting others – instead, it gives a sense of the lesser status of all of wretched humanity.

At present, our beneficial meetings with the Sublime occur pretty much at random. One just happens to see an amazing sunset or chances to look out of the window of the plane when it's passing over the Dolomites or the Taurus mountains. But this doesn't tie in with an understanding of the place of the Sublime in our emotional lives – if we see what it can do for us, we shouldn't leave that to chance, we should be strategic and 'make appointments' with deserts, glaciers and oceans on a regular basis.

We've got a model for how to do this – though it comes in a slightly unfortunate guise. Religions have often ensured that their followers would meet with the Sublime on a weekly basis, in a cathedral or church somewhere not very far from where they lived. They constructed buildings specifically designed to awe the congregation. But they didn't just hope that people would drop by. They put a date in the diary, every week.

If you lived in the Vienna suburb of Wieden, for instance, you'd go to the Karlskirche at 11.00am every Sunday and be confronted with the Sublime. This beneficial psychological service is in reality distinct from the specifically religious convictions that orchestrated it. But the decline of organised religious faith in many parts of the world has inadvertently also taken away this collective commitment to regularly reactivating our sense of the Sublime.

One potential source of the Sublime is travel. And in fact, at a key point in history, the search for the Sublime provided a central motive for the invention of the modern travel industry. When the idea of overseas holidays got going in the 19th century, its focus was not (as it became in the 20th century) sunbathing; rather, the most popular destination was the Alps – and a desire to be awed. This idea of what travel was about was the consequence of a long campaign of artistic and poetic works praising the Sublime character of the mountains and their power to calm the mind.

The visitors didn't want to climb the peaks. They wanted to gaze at them from the surrounding valleys. Many were following the advice of the poet Shelley. In July 1816, he visited the Chamonix valley near Geneva with his wife Mary and her stepsister Claire. They stayed at the Hotel de Londres and Shelley particularly enjoyed walking on the bridge over the nearby river Arve. In one poem he describes standing on the bridge and lifting his eyes higher and higher, above the cataracts and the wooded hills and the lower bands of clouds until 'Far, far above, piercing the infinite sky, Mont Blanc appears'. The sight of its noble grandeur, he said, makes the beholder think of the fundamental issues in life. It corrects our scale of values. Guided by Shelley, later visitors weren't travelling simply to see the sights, but in order to transform their inner lives by a Sublime encounter with ancient granite. The external journey was undertaken in support of an inner journey of development.

We do in fact often continue to travel in search of calm today. Many resorts advertise themselves on the basis of their ability to soothe the body – and they promote the idea that the primary way to achieve tranquillity is via rest and physical comfort. But the big theme that excited earlier travellers isn't fully exploited at the moment. And that's because it's founded on the currently less familiar idea of attaining calm via an encounter with a new scale. It's the view that we might be agitated not simply because we are tired but because we have the wrong perspective on the events in our lives – and that therefore the kind of travel that would benefit us would need to promote a better sense of scale.

Traditionally, another of the major sources of the consoling perspective of the Sublime has been the sight of the sky at night. People would look up from the troubled surface of the earth and find consolation in their impression of the rational, beautiful order of the heavens. The ancient Greeks and Romans, for instance, linked their divinities to the lights they saw in the night sky, which we now know to be planets and which we continue to call by the names by which the ancients worshipped them: Mercury, Venus, Mars, Jupiter and the rest.

It is a line of thought that has persisted in one version or another for a very long time. In the late 18th century, for instance, the German philosopher Immanuel Kant thought the sight of 'the starry heavens above' was the most Sublime spectacle in nature and that contemplation of this transcendent sight could hugely assist us in coping with the travails of everyday life.

Although Kant was interested in the developing science of astronomy, he still saw the stars as serving a major psychological purpose. Unfortunately, since then, the advances in astrophysics have become increasingly embarrassed around this aspect of the stars. It would seem deeply odd today if in a science class there were a special section not on the fact that Aldebaran is an orange-red giant star of spectral and luminosity type K5 III and that it is currently losing mass at a rate of $(1–1.6) \times 10^{-11}$ $M\odot \ yr^{-1}$ with a velocity of 30km $s^{-1}$, but rather on the ways in which the sight of stars can help us manage our emotional lives and relations with our families. This is true even though knowing how to cope better with anxiety is in most lives a more urgent and important task than steering one's space rocket around the galaxies. Although we've made vast scientific progress since Kant's time, we haven't properly explored the potential of space as a source of wisdom, as opposed to a puzzle for astrophysicists to unpick.

On an evening walk, you look up and see the planets Venus and Jupiter shining in the darkening sky. If the dusk deepens, you might see some stars – the constellation of Orion and many others. It's a hint of the unimaginable extensions of space across the solar system, the galaxy, the cosmos. They were there, quietly revolving, their light streaming down as spotted hyenas warily eyed a Stone Age village and as Julius Caesar's triremes set out after midnight to cross the Channel and see the cliffs of

England at dawn. The sight has a calming effect because none of our troubles, disappointments or hopes have any relevance. Everything that happens to us, or that we do, is of no consequence whatever from the point of view of the universe.

## iv. Time

It seems almost disrespectful to ask what the point might be of bothering with history. History is one of the most prestigious and long-established topics of study. Without really thinking about it, we naturally assume that it must be good for us to know about the past – though the precise nature of the benefit is rarely spelled out. Those responsible for the government of nations might draw practical guidance about avoiding war on two fronts simultaneously or the consequence of over-rapid industrialisation. But what benefit for personal existence might be extracted from engagement with the distant past?

One important use we can make of history is to resort to it as an antidote to anxiety and panic. And we might do this, for instance, by turning to the writings of the ancient Roman historian Suetonius.

Born towards the end of the 1st century AD, Gaius Suetonius Tranquillus worked for many years at the top levels of the imperial administration, rising to the position of chief secretary to the emperor Hadrian. He was the first historian to try to give a fairly accurate portrait of what the rulers of the empire were actually like. In *The Twelve Caesars,* he provides a summary of their achievements from Julius Caesar down to Domitian – who reigned until AD 96, by which point Suetonius himself was in his twenties. He then records insider views on what these people had actually been like to work for and how they had behaved in private. He had access to the archives and was personal friends with many of those who had served in senior positions.

In the book, Suetonius quietly catalogues the follies and crimes of the first twelve men to rule the Western world. Among them:

*Julius Caesar:* 'Caesar stood for the office of pontifex maximus, and used the most flagrant bribery to secure it.'

*Caligula:* 'Many men of decent family were branded at his command and sent down the mines, or put to work on the roads, or thrown to the wild beasts. Others were confined in narrow cages, where they had to crouch on all fours like animals, or were sawn in half – and not necessarily for major offences, but merely for criticising his shows, failing to swear by his genius, and so forth.'

'The method of execution he preferred was to inflict numerous small wounds, avoiding the prisoner's vital organs, and his familiar order "Make him feel that he is dying!" soon became proverbial.'

*Nero:* 'He was released from a den dressed in the skins of wild animals, and attacked the private parts of men and women who stood bound to stakes.'

'One of his games was to attack men on their way home from dinner, stab them if they offered resistance, and then drop their bodies down the sewers.'

*Vitellius:* 'Vitellius' ruling vices were gluttony and cruelty. He banqueted three and often four times a day, namely morning, noon, afternoon and evening – the last meal being mainly a drinking bout – and survived the ordeal well enough by vomiting frequently.'

'His cruelty was such that he would kill or torture anyone at all on the slightest pretext'.

*Domitian:* 'At the beginning of his reign Domitian would spend hours alone every day doing nothing more than catching flies and stabbing them with a needle-sharp pen.'

Though Suetonius writes about grotesque people – who were also at the time the most powerful people on the planet – and about horrific events, reading him can leave one feeling remarkably serene. One might flick through the pages sitting at an airport, crunching an apple and sublimating the frustration of a delayed plane. Or perhaps tucked up in bed, after a fierce row with one's partner. The experience could be strangely relaxing. It seems paradoxical, because Suetonius is ostensibly merely providing us with a record of some deeply disreputable actions. And yet the effect is to leave us feeling more comfortable and more relaxed, less pent up about our own day-to-day issues or resentful about our humiliations.

One reason the study of history can help us be calmer is that it tends to be a narrative of resilience. Caligula and Nero were catastrophically bad leaders. Suetonius writes of earthquakes, plagues, wars, riots, rebellions, conspiracies, betrayals, coups and mass slaughter. Considered on its own it seems to be the record of a society that is utterly corrupt and incompetent, that is so rotten its total collapse must surely be imminent. But in fact Suetonius was writing before – and not after – the most impressive period of Roman achievement – which would come fifty years later under the rule of the Stoic philosopher and emperor, Marcus Aurelius.

Very strangely, as it turns out, these are not the annals of a society that is falling apart. They are the stories of genuinely awful things that were compatible with a society heading overall towards peace and prosperity. Reading Suetonius suggests that it is not fatal for societies to be in trouble; it is usual for things to go rather badly. In this respect, reading ancient history generates the opposite emotions to scanning today's news. The news machine is based on the idea of getting us agitated. News is always trying to tell us that something entirely new and very alarming is occurring: there's a wholly original health risk, international conflict, threat to global stability or risk to the economy. Whereas Suetonius would be deeply unperturbed. The news has been much worse before and things were, in the end, OK. People behaving very badly is a normal state of affairs. It was ever thus: there have always been disappointing leaders and greedy magnates. There have always been existential threats to the human race and civilisation. It makes no sense, and is a form of twisted narcissism, to imagine that our era has any kind of monopoly on perversity or chaos. Suetonius would never be shocked by modern scandal because he'd heard so much worse before. By reading him, we enter unconsciously into his less agitated and more stoic reactions.

On a grand scale, this explains why grandparents typically have a calmer approach to bringing up children than parents do. The grandparents have a more accurate grasp of how normal – and therefore less alarming – many problems are. Their calm is based on two key bits of knowledge. They know that whatever is done, one's children will turn out very far from perfect – and therefore the intensely agitating worry that one might be making a mistake is usually a bit misplaced. But they also grasp that even when things go a bit wrong, children will generally cope well enough. Their sense of danger and their sense of hope have both been made more accurate by experience. History encourages the less panicky sides of ourselves.

In the 18th century, Edward Gibbon wrote a monumental study entitled *The History of the Decline and Fall of the Roman Empire.* He was deeply influenced by Suetonius and came to the view that 'History is, indeed, little more than the register of the crimes, follies, and misfortune of mankind.' He starts out by evoking the power, security and massive extent of the Roman Empire in its period of greatest strength. Across seven volumes, he then describes error, disaster, collapse and failure on the largest possible scale – and in so doing he discovers a further source of tranquillity.

It took many centuries for Rome to fall. Gibbon covers a vast sweep of events, and he movingly notes that most events, however huge they seem at the time, 'leave a faint impression on the page of history'. Everything gets forgotten. The same will happen to us – and to our troubles. The way of ordering things, which seems so essential and important to us, will eventually become bizarre and outmoded. History functions as a corrective. It gains its power because it balances out the more self-centred of our preoccupations. It restores us when the present seems as if it is all that there is.

Gibbon himself was a remarkably sedate and dispassionate figure, who spent much of his life sitting quietly at his desk able to cope admirably with the tribulations of his life – he got on badly with his father, he was unable to marry the person he wanted to, and he suffered for years from a swollen testicle. He was calm not despite recounting the horrors of the past and the evidence that everything comes eventually to ruin – but because he knew and loved the past so well.

## v. Touch

Although it wasn't always so, for a long time now, people have been broadly willing to accept that sex is one of the legitimate needs of the body. Today it is pretty well understood that not getting enough sex can be a real problem, leading to feelings of stress, disconnection and difficulties with concentration. But there's another area of physical need that's not, as yet, fully appreciated. It's the idea that when you are feeling agitated and anxious, what you might really need is a hug. There's little opposition to hugs in general, but we're collectively reluctant to see them as addressing serious emotional requirements.

Hugs are associated primarily with the very young. Up to about the age of four, a child may be frequently hugged and held, cradled, patted and carried. We accept that a little person can't manage everything on their own. There will be times when they need a big person to look after them, support them, keep them safe and fed and comfortable – and calm them down with a hug. Being physically enfolded in a parent's arms may partially recreate the ultimate stress-free environment: the womb. The young child can't be helped by explanations and reasons; they respond to touch: gentle warm pressure soothes and relaxes the body and quiets the agitated mind.

However, a hug cannot really be entirely understood just in physical terms. Its power to comfort and console is bound up with the wordless promises it conveys. The true hug is an offer of protection. The arms that embrace the child will defend it against whatever it dreads and will keep it safe in the face of all the dangers that haunt its imagination.

When a hug is most genuine it is also the outward gesture that indicates a readiness to be gentle in terms of understanding the other. The hug implies that one will go slowly and easily, one will not judge negatively, one will be patient in finding out what is genuinely the matter, one will see everything in the kindliest light: sympathy is guaranteed, forgiveness will be available if needed. It is the offer of adult wisdom in the face of immature woes, where the adult will be able to see through the confusion, put things right, teach, assist and solve the problem in a good way. When a parent hugs a child, it is an intimation of an ability to mend broken things. Like a great work of art, a hug is the sensory embodiment of important ideas, an outward sign of inward generosity. And though we might never put any of this into words, it is a source of applied wisdom.

But as the child grows towards adulthood, the assumptions shift dramatically. Independence and self-reliance are central to the ideals of adulthood. We become very wary of any suggestion of needing a wiser, stronger person to look after us. We get prickly around any hint that we might be being patronised or condescended to. One of our most taboo political ideas is paternalism – the admission of a collective desire to be parented, which is taken to be profoundly humiliating.

In this emotional environment, it becomes difficult to take the need for hugs seriously. Hugging can come to seem merely an interesting, elective social style: an expansive alternative to a handshake, which is friendly enough, of course, but doesn't express anything like the full vision of kindness that was there in the best hugs of childhood.

To suggest that someone requires a hug is to say something potentially, but only potentially, demeaning. It's suggesting that they are, at least for the moment, rather like a child. They have the same kinds of emotional needs that we come to think of as essentially childlike. To need a hug is to admit that one is incapable of coping on one's own, that one requires protection, guidance, the help of someone wiser and more capable, that one needs to have one's troubles and anxieties reinterpreted by a more mature mind. It is to say, in shorthand, 'I am at the moment like a child and I need someone else to be, for a while, like a parent.'

Yet even if we don't usually like to admit it, there are in fact many times when we should be able to revert to a childlike position. There are moments of adult life when one seems petulant, scared, shy and sure that everything suddenly feels totally unfair. One's ability to look after oneself is terribly depleted. At such times, to get ourselves back together, we need someone else to take the burden from us. We require the equivalent of what the parent does for the child. We are in need of someone to pat us on the head, to put us to bed early, tuck us in and hold us tight.

It's tricky to admit how normal and actually reasonable regressive tendencies are; they are an affront to individualism and dignity. They can be cast as pathetic and self-indulgent. It's awkward to acknowledge that they exist in someone who is 1m 74cm tall and has a day job as a dental hygienist or commercial litigation specialist.

It is – therefore – very helpful to come across profoundly dignified and prestigious cultural objects that take the need for hugs very seriously indeed. In a late work, the *Mystic Nativity*, Sandro Botticelli (who was a great observer of the parent–child hug) shows some angels hugging adult humans.

Sandro Botticelli, *Mystic Nativity* (detail), c.1500

Botticelli was hugely sensitive to the way in which failure and fear are always edging their way into every life – irrespective of how sunny it might look from the outside. The hug is not – for an adult – going to make everything better. But it acknowledges that the strong person will inevitably at times feel like a child and that this should not be met with contempt but with infinite sweetness and warmth.

The periodic need to regress should be seen not as a sign of a failure of maturity but as an aspect of a wise adult acceptance of one's own deep imperfection and ultimate inadequacy. It can be interpreted as a frank admission that one has taken on too much. Regressing can signal a legitimate need for assistance that has gone unmet for too long, because asking for certain kinds of help has been stigmatised. We live in a competitive environment that makes failure frequent and yet terrifying. We have high expectations and anxieties around body mass index, family life, global security, personal hygiene, never being able to afford to retire, fuel consumption, disposable income, the health risks attached to a food one likes, home-ownership, decluttering, child-development milestones, hotel upgrades, KPIs, quarterly targets ... Regression doesn't involve renouncing these concerns. But it may be a very sane pause as one carries the burdens.

In kinder, more mature relationships, we'd make allowances for each other's occasional times of regression. Part of what it is to love another person is to be accommodating and generous to these needs. Ideally, the strange behaviour around regression is itself a sign that someone feels safe enough with you (or you with them) to be pathetic for a time. To love another person isn't only to admire their strengths and see what's great about them. It should also involve nursing and protecting them in their less impressive moments. To ask for a hug is not simply to request a physical embrace. It has a bigger meaning as an admission that one is not coping and as a plea for protection and support. A hug is a symbol of what we are missing in our hypercompetitive, individualistic culture: a positive admission of our dependence and fragility.

# Conclusion

## The Quiet Life

It would be nice to think that it would be possible to eventually achieve deep and permanent calm. But this hope can itself become a source of agitation. Setting our sights on a very appealing – but actually unreachable – goal leads to frustration and disappointment. The greater the investment in the ideal of unruffled peace of mind, the more upsetting any failure of poise becomes. It's painful, of course, but there's also a comic side to the clash between hope and what actually tends to happen: the yoga master who has spent years pursuing serenity in an isolated monastery setting off to demonstrate their poise to the world and getting stressed and deranged at the airport when their luggage fails to appear on the carousel. It isn't their suffering that's funny. We're laughing with relief at the reminder that getting agitated isn't simply a personal failing of our own; it's a universal and unavoidable part of the human condition.

We should never seek the total elimination of anxiety. We carry too many sources of stubborn agitation inside us. Beyond any specific thing we happen to be worrying about, looked at over time, a stern conclusion is inescapable: we simply are often anxious, to our core, in the very basic make-up of our being. Though we may focus day-to-day on this or that particular worry creating static in our minds, what we are really up against is anxiety as a permanent feature of life, something irrevocable, existential, dogged – and responsible for ruining a dominant share of our brief time on earth. Tortured by anxiety, we naturally fall prey to powerful fantasies about what might – finally – bring us calm. At certain points, especially in the north, the fantasies latch on to travel. On a sunny island, at last, there would be peace: under the clear blue sky, on the island eleven-and-a-half hours from here, seven time zones away, with the warm water lapping at our feet, and with access to a seaside villa on pontoons, with Egyptian cotton sheets and a refreshing breeze. It is just a matter of holding on for a few more months – and parting with an extraordinary sum.

Or perhaps we would be calm if the house could be as we really want it: with everything in its place, no more clutter, pristine walls, ample cupboards, stripped oak, limestone, recessed lighting and a bank of new appliances.

Or perhaps we will be calm when one day we reach the right place in the company, or the novel is sold, or the film is made or our shares are worth £5 billion – and we can walk into a room of strangers and they will know at once.

Or (and this one we keep a little more to ourselves) there might be calm if we had the right sort of person in our lives, someone who could properly understand us, a creature with whom it wouldn't be so difficult, who would be kind and playfully sympathetic, who would have thoughtful, compassionate eyes and in whose arms we could lie in peace, almost like a child – though not quite.

Travel, Beauty, Status and Love: the four great contemporary ideals around which our fantasies of calm collect and that taken together are responsible for the lion's share of the frenzied activities of the modern economy: its airports, long-haul jets and resort hotels; its overheated property markets, furniture companies and unscrupulous building contractors; its networking events, status-driven media and competitive business deals; its bewitching actors, soaring love songs and busy divorce lawyers.

Yet despite the promises and the passion expended in the pursuit of these goals, none of them will work. There will be anxiety at the beach, in the pristine home, after the sale of the company, and in the arms of anyone we will ever seduce, however often we try.

Anxiety is our fundamental state for well-founded reasons:

- Because we are intensely vulnerable physical beings, a complicated network of fragile organs all biding their time before eventually letting us down catastrophically at a moment of their own choosing.

- Because we have insufficient information upon which to make most major life decisions: we are steering more or less blind.

- Because we can imagine so much more than we have and live in mobile-driven, mediatised societies where envy and restlessness will be a constant.

- Because we are the descendants of the great worriers of the species, the others having been trampled and torn apart by wild animals, and because we still carry in our bones – into the calm of the suburbs – the terrors of the savannah.

- Because the progress of our careers and of our finances play themselves out within the tough-minded, competitive, destructive, random workings of an uncontained capitalist engine.

- Because we rely for our self-esteem and sense of comfort on the love of people we cannot control and whose needs and hopes will never align seamlessly with our own.

All of which is not to say that there aren't better and worse ways to approach our condition.

The single most important move is acceptance. There is no need – on top of everything else – to be anxious that we are anxious. The mood is no sign that our lives have gone wrong, merely that we are alive.

We should spare ourselves the burden of loneliness. We are far from the only ones with this problem. Everyone is more anxious than they are inclined to tell us. Even the tycoon and the couple in love are suffering. We've collectively failed to admit to ourselves what we are truly like.

We must learn to laugh about our anxieties – laughter being the exuberant expression of relief when a hitherto private agony is given a well-crafted social formulation in a joke. We must suffer alone. But we can at least hold out our arms to our similarly tortured, fractured, and above all else, anxious neighbours, as if to say, in the kindest way possible: 'I know …'

A calm life isn't one that's always perfectly serene. It is one where we are committed to calming down more readily, and where we strive for more realistic expectations; where we can understand better why certain problems are occurring, and we can be more adept at finding a consoling perspective. The progress is painfully limited and imperfect – but it is genuine.

The more calm matters to us, the more we will be aware of all the very many times when we have been less calm than we might have been. We'll be sensitive to our own painfully frequent bouts of irritation and upset. It can feel laughably hypocritical. Surely a genuine devotion to calm would mean ongoing serenity? But this isn't really a fair judgement to make, because being calm all the time isn't a viable option. What counts is the commitment one is making to the idea of being calmer. You can count legitimately as a lover of calm when you ardently want to be calm, not when you succeed at being calm on all occasions. However frequent the lapses, the devotion counts as real.

Furthermore, it's a psychological law that those who are most attracted to calm will also – in all probability – be especially irritable and by nature prone to particularly high levels of anxiety. We've got a mistaken picture of what the lover of calm looks like; we assume them to be among the most tranquil of the species. We're working with the highly misleading background assumption that the lover of something is the person who is really good at it. But the person who loves something is the one who is hugely aware of how much they lack it. And, therefore, of how much they need it.

It's the same general psychological law that's at work in a strange fact about art history – identified by the German philosopher Wilhelm Worringer in his essay *Abstraction and Empathy* (1907). Worringer focused attention on periods of great social and cultural agitation that were, at the same time, especially interested in calm works. For example, the huge, serene Blue Mosque in Istanbul was built in the first decades of the 16th century, precisely when the Ottoman Empire was involved in multiple wars. The building project was in fact initiated following an especially severe military defeat. The huge interior spaces were covered with delicately abstract tiles in flowing patterns that have a deeply calming effect. Worringer argued that the Ottomans were drawn to this kind of architecture because these were the qualities lacking in their actual lives. Admiration for calm isn't an expression of one's existing ability to be serene. The longing to be calm can be a deeply significant and precious part of one's character, especially when turmoil grips the mind. If you pay attention only to someone's active behaviour, you're engaging with only a narrow slice of how they are. It is their longings you need to see or imagine. Despite having slammed the door, felt enraged, cursed and had a bout of anxiety, one can still be an authentic and honourable lover of calm.

Our culture is very willing to pay lip service to calm. We certainly don't despise it. But equally we don't really see calm as being a particularly important ingredient in a good life. Hence the fact that the idea of living a quiet – or calm – life has, when we really drill into it, a far from entirely positive ring to it. To say that someone is opting for a quiet life is often a way of gently chiding them for giving up on the more arduous but more serious, and ideally more rewarding, challenges of existence. We tend to associate having a quiet time with resting, recovering from an illness or with retirement. In other words, you opt for a quiet life only when you are not up to coping with the other, more exciting, possibilities. But this isn't an accurate reflection of the role of calm in our lives. Keeping relatively calm is a central precondition for managing well enough in many areas of existence. The quiet life isn't a climbdown – it often more accurately tracks how we need to live in order to flourish.

The thing that our society has invested in most, as the key ingredient of a good life, is money. We are always being re-minded of the links between having more money and increas-ing satisfaction. What's not always so clear in our minds is that the process of acquiring money has a range of built-in psycho-logical opportunity costs that we too easily ignore. We pay for our wealth with broken nights, fractious relationships, distant family ties – at times, with life itself. We should look not only at the money we have accumulated, but also at the calm that we have forfeited while doing so.

Our society is eloquent on the advantages of money; it pays desperately little attention to the advantages of bypassing cer-tain opportunities to make it, especially in terms of the calm that might be gained.

It's hard for most of us to contemplate any potential in the idea of a quiet life because the defenders of such lives have tended to come from the most implausible sections of the community: slackers, hippies, the work-shy, the fired ... peo-ple who seem like they have never had a choice about how to arrange their affairs. A quiet life seems like something im-posed upon them by their own ineptitude. It is a pitiable con-solation prize.

And yet, when we examine matters closely, busy lives turn out to have certain strikingly high incidental costs that we are nevertheless collectively committed to ignoring. Visible success brings us up against the envy and competitiveness of strangers.

We become plausible targets for disappointment and spite; it can seem as if it may be our fault that certain others have not succeeded. Winning higher status makes us increasingly sensitive to its loss; we start to note every possible new snub. A slight decrease in sales, attention or adulation can feel like a catastrophe. Our health suffers. We fall prey to scared, paranoid thoughts; we see possible plots everywhere, and we may not be wrong. The threat of vindictive scandal haunts us. Alongside our privileges, we grow impoverished in curious ways. We have very limited control over our time.

We may be able to shut down a factory in India, and our every word is listened to with trembling respect within the organisation, but what we absolutely cannot do is admit that we are also extremely tired and just want to spend the afternoon reading on the sofa. We can no longer express our more spontaneous, imaginative, vulnerable sides. Our words are so consequential, we have to be guarded at all times; others are looking to us for guidance and authority. Along the way, we become strangers to those who love us outside of our wealth and status – while depending ever more on the fickle attention of those for whom we are our achievements alone. Our children see ever less of us. Our spouses grow bitter. We may own the wealth of continents, but it has been ten years at least since we last had the chance to do nothing for a day.

The most famous cultural figure in the history of the West was very interested in the benefits that can attend quiet lives. In Mark 6: 8–9, Jesus tells his disciples 'to take nothing for their journey except a staff – no bread, no bag, no money in their belts – but to wear sandals and not put on two tunics'. Christianity opens up vital space in our imaginations by making a distinction between two kinds of poverty: what it terms voluntary poverty on the one hand and involuntary poverty on the other. We are at this point in history so deeply fixated on the idea that poverty must always be involuntary and therefore the result of a lack of talent and indigence, we can't even imagine that it might be the result of an intelligent and skilled person's free choice based on a rational evaluation of costs and benefits. It might sincerely be possible for someone to decide not to take the better-paid job, not to publish another book, not to seek high office – and to do so not because they had no chance, but because – having surveyed the externalities involved – they chose not to fight for them.

One of the central moments in Christian history came in 1204 when a wealthy young man we know today as St Francis of Assisi willingly renounced his worldly goods, of which he had quite a few (a couple of houses, a farm and a ship at least). He did so not through any external compulsion. He just felt they would interfere with other things he really wanted rather more of: a chance to contemplate Jesus's teachings, to honour the creator of the earth, to admire the flowers and the trees – and to help the poorest in society.

Chinese culture has also been reverent towards the *yinshi* (recluse); someone who chooses to leave behind the busy political and commercial world and live more simply, usually up the side of a mountain – in a hut. The tradition began in the 4th century AD, when a high-ranking government official named Tao Yuanming surrendered his position at court and moved to the countryside to farm the land, make wine and write. In his poem, 'On Drinking Wine', he recounts the riches that poverty has brought him:

Plucking chrysanthemums from the eastern hedge
I gaze into the distance at the southern mountain.
The mountain air is refreshing at sunset
As the flocking birds are returning home.
In such things we find true meaning,
But when I try to explain, I can't find the words.

Portraits of Tao Yuanming became a major theme in Chinese art and literature. His hut near Mount Lushan ('Hut Mountain') gave others encouragement to see the advantages of cheaper, simpler dwellings. A number of poets of the Tang dynasty went through periods of seclusion. Bai Juyi (772–846) wrote a poem lovingly describing the hut he'd bought himself on the edge of a forest, listing its plain and natural materials (a thatched roof with 'stone steps, cassia pillars, and a fence of plaited bamboo'). The poet Du Fu, living in Chengdu in the Sichuan province, wrote a poem titled 'My Thatched Hut Ruined by the Autumn Wind'. It wasn't a lament, more a celebration of the freedom that came with living so simply that a storm might blow over your house.

There are for many of us plenty of options to take up certain career paths that carry high prestige with them. We could have something deeply impressive to answer those who ask us what we do. But this does not necessarily mean we must or should follow these possibilities. When we come to know the true price some careers exact, we may slowly realise we are not willing to pay for the ensuing envy, fear, deceit and anxiety. Our days are limited on the earth. We may – for the sake of true riches – willingly, and with no loss of dignity, opt to become a little poorer and more obscure.

In theory, we can just take a purely personal and private decision to opt for a quiet life, if that's what we want. We don't need to seek the approval of others. We don't need to care too much whether other people share our attitudes. We'd like to think that we're genuinely independent. But in practice it actually makes a huge difference if we feel that what we are doing is normal (in the sense that a lot of other people can be expected to see the point and to approve) or a bit odd (in the sense that it attracts surprised attention, or even disapproval). We are in truth very much social animals, which means that we endlessly absorb cues about what is important and what's not from what most people around us are doing. It doesn't apply very strictly absolutely all the time – of course – but overall our sense of what's normal is a powerful shaping force on our own behaviour and thinking. A lot of our devotion to money and activity is socially determined. We don't just emerge from the womb as natural seekers after corporate careers or holidays in the Caribbean. We learn our life priorities, our picture of success and the targets of our ambition from others. If we are ever to balance that out, we're going to need the same level of cultural help.

Ideally there would be a strong, collective recognition that the pursuit of calm plays a big, central role in a good life. But as yet we don't have this. Our public vision of success is still excessively focused on stimulation and excitement. For this change to happen we need a culture that provides a strong endorsement of the value of a quiet life and of the things that contribute to it. What we call culture – though it sounds strange initially to put it this way – is essentially the advertising and promotion of ideas. Culture suggests a script for how to live, how to think, what to consider important or trivial. It gives us a picture of what's admirable and what's not. Western culture has not, on the whole – in recent decades – been especially devoted to the promotion of calm. We need many more great, eloquent and prestigious statements of the attractions of the quiet life. In a calm Utopia, major films, hit songs and hugely popular video games would centre around modesty, patience and the appreciation of small pleasures. At the moment, this sounds a bit fanciful because we have got a vision of popularity that's closely bound up with excitement.

But, in theory, it can't be impossible to build high levels of attraction for quiet things – it's just more difficult. The emergence of this skill is one of the keys to the development of a calmer culture and hence of easing the individual task of getting a calmer life. It's a fantasy, of course, but it points in an important direction. And we hope that this book – which you are about to close – is a modest but real contribution in the direction of more serene lives.

# Credits

p. 10    Pillows by Jay Mantri, Creative Commons License, www.jaymantri.com,
         http://jaymantri.com/post/120742882173/.

p. 42    Urban Crowd from Above © George Clerk, www.georgeclerk.com, iStock

p. 64    *Moving Out* by Dave Kleinschmidt. Flickr / Creative Commons License
         www.flickr.com/photos/dklein/534251317/sizes/o/.

p. 84    *Wall Glow* by Emdot. Flickr / Creative Commons License
         www.flickr.com/photos/emdot/6101065/.

p. 86    Ryōan-ji Temple Zen rock garden in the spring, Kyoto, Japan.
         © Sean Pavone / Alamy Stock Photo.

p. 86    Buddha figure. © Lasse Kristensen / Alamy Stock Photo.

p. 89    Santa Maria Monastery, monks' dormitory, Alcobaca, Estremadura and
         Ribatejo Province, Portugal. © GM Photo Images / Alamy Stock Photo.

p. 91    Claude Lorrain, *Landscape with Hagar and the Angel*, 1646.
         © Heritage Image Partnership Ltd / Alamy Stock Photo.

p. 92    Martin, Agnes (1912–2004): *Stone*, 1964. New York, Museum of Modern
         Art (MoMA). Ink on paper, 10 7/8 x 10 7/8" (27.7 x 27.7 cm). Eugene
         and Clare Thaw Fund. Acc. no.: 606.1964. © 2016. Digital image, The
         Museum of Modern Art, New York/Scala, Florence. © Agnes Martin /
         DACS 2016.

p. 94    View of the interior of the palace church at Hartenfels Palace in Torgau,
         Germany. Photo: Peter Endig / dpa / Alamy Live News. © dpa picture
         alliance / Alamy Stock Photo

p. 94    Italy, Veneto, Venice, Church Of Santa Maria Gloriosa Dei Frari. © Hemis
         / Alamy Stock Photo

p. 119   Sandro Botticelli, *Mystic Nativity*, c.1500. © INTERFOTO /
         Alamy Stock Photo.

p. 122   Ocean by Jay Mantri, Creative Commons License, www.jaymantri.com,
         www.pexels.com/photo/wave-ocean-5350/.

**The School of Life** is dedicated to developing emotional intelligence – believing that our most persistent problems are created by a lack of self-understanding, compassion and communication. We operate from ten physical campuses around the world, including London, Amsterdam, Seoul and Melbourne. We produce films, run classes, offer therapy and make a range of psychological products. **The School of Life Press** publishes books on the most important issues of emotional life. Our titles are designed to entertain, educate, console and transform.